FROM BEAT DOWN
TO BACK UP AND BEYOND

From
BEAT DOWN to
BACK UP and
BEYOND

How a Suicidal Addict Achieved Success
Against All the Odds *(And How You Can Too...)*

JAMES NEVILLE-TAYLOR

HOUNDSTOOTH
PRESS

FROM BEAT DOWN TO BACK UP AND BEYOND
How a Suicidal Addict Achieved Success Against All the Odds
(And How You Can Too...)

FIRST EDITION

ISBN 978-1-5445-4248-5 Hardcover
      978-1-5445-4247-8 Paperback
      978-1-5445-4246-1 Ebook

*This book is dedicated to
every single person suffering in silence.
To those who feel alone and think they
have nowhere else to turn.*

*It is dedicated to everyone who is
no longer with us due to feeling so alone and lost,
they didn't want to be here anymore.*

*To those still with us, may this book help you
to see there is nothing to be ashamed of
and nothing you can't talk about.*

*My aim for this book is to help break
the stigma around mental health problems
and suicidal thoughts.*

*If it can reach just one person who is struggling,
inspiring them to try again and reach out
to talk to someone, then it
has done its job.*

Contents

PART 1
THE PATH TO ROCK BOTTOM

PART 2
CLIMBING MY WAY OUT

Foreword

By Rachel Pedersen, "Queen of Social Media,"
CEO of The Viral Touch digital marketing agency,
and Founder of Social Media United

Throughout life, all of us struggle. For some, it's difficult to pursue their dreams and go for success. Others struggle with day-to-day functioning. I know firsthand what it's like to struggle with mental health, let alone while building a business. Every single day can be incredibly intense (hello, struggle bus)!

I've been in business less than a decade and have had a lot of success by most standards. We've done over $10 million in revenue, have millions of followers, and have won all the awards. But what most people don't see are the days I don't even want to get out of bed.

It's always been a desire of mine to see other people open up about these types of struggles, especially among successful entrepreneurs. Maybe then, I finally wouldn't feel so alone in my struggles.

I had the privilege of experiencing someone opening up about exactly this.

Four years ago, I was invited to attend a Mastermind event in sunny Los Angeles. There were people from across the world in that intimate gathering with incredible insights.

Among the members of the group was one person who sat quietly at first. He didn't raise his hand much and seemed to just be listening intently while taking notes. My immediate assumption was that he was incredibly kind but quite reserved.

However, the moment it was his turn to get up in front and share, he came to life. I was absolutely blown away by what he shared for the next half hour. All of us in the room cried, laughed, and were incredibly inspired by this man's story.

That man was James Neville-Taylor.

James shared his life story with us, and I was not prepared for how incredibly vulnerable he was with it. In his vulnerability was a strength that surprised me. He had this quiet calm to him, and his story captivated me. Nearly everyone in the room was crying: we were absolutely moved by each twist and turn of his life. We were emotional listening to it all, and it was wild to wrap my brain around the fact that James had lived it!

But then he began to share with us about business, and it lit a fire under my butt! If he had struggled just to live and was still able to pursue his dreams, I knew I could too.

James is unique in that he's humbly brilliant. Every time he shares his wisdom related to business and motivation, I have to stop and listen. So when he sent me his book and asked me to write the foreword, it was an absolute honor. "Yes!" I blurted out, practically before he finished the question. Reading the book revitalized the feelings from the LA Mastermind as he shared his stories in even more vivid detail on the page.

Reading this book will be a catalyst for your success as you laugh, cry, and experience the motivation of taking on your dreams.

Enjoy James's brilliance, my friends.

Preface

In 2017, I wanted to die.

I overdosed and waited for my life to be over.

Since that fateful moment, I've built my own multimillion-dollar business, spoken on stages around the world, mentored thousands of clients, pulled myself and my entire family out of poverty, and done things I never thought possible a few short years ago.

Why am I telling you this?

I know what it's like to be at the bottom of the barrel, wanting to end it all. I am a huge advocate for mental health, and I know my story has transformed lives. You may think you are stuck where you are and won't be able to change. Yet I am living proof you can.

You can survive all manner of abuse, neglect, pain, sadness, and humiliation—and *still* thrive. You name it, I've probably been through it, survived it, and thrived after it. We are stronger than we know.

I know this firsthand from being in the worst pain of my life and wanting to end it all. I went from thinking there was no way anything could get any worse to finding a place even lower and darker than I could imagine. Yet I survived it all and came out the other side stronger than ever.

If you think you have been pushed to your limit and have nothing left to give, chances are you are wrong. We humans instinctively shy away from pain, and when it descends on us anyway, our minds tell us we can't take it anymore. But there is strength in the low place: it's where we find out who we truly are and what we're capable of. As much as I wouldn't wish my struggles on my worst enemy, they made me resilient and able to handle emotional stresses that would cause most people to crumble.

My mother, on the other hand, was sheltered well into her twenties. If something went wrong, my grandparents were always there to pick up the pieces, and she always had someone to fall back on if it "got too much." This meant she wasn't well equipped for a child at twenty-one years of age, and she certainly wasn't prepared for the years that lay ahead.

I blamed my mother for a lot of things growing up, but I've come to learn you can't blame people for the way they were raised. We all make mistakes, and I no longer blame her for hers: she played the cards she was dealt as well as she could. In the same way, she can't blame me for the demonic little brat I became because of how I was raised. We are all by-products of our upbringing, and we either become very similar to our parents or polar opposites.

Until, that is, we begin our second life.

I believe we have two lives. The first is the sheltered life, blissfully ignorant and unaware. The second life begins when we reach our lowest point, whatever that may be. This lowest point is the pivotal moment in which we stop being victims of circumstances and allowing external things to shape us. This is the moment we begin living a life by design.

I've arguably lived a difficult life, but I wouldn't trade it with someone who has lived a sheltered life because I am so much more prepared to cope with what lies ahead. We all have hardships in life: loss, abuse, and disappointment, to name a few. It's the way we deal with these struggles and come out the other side that defines us.

Today, I'm a self-made millionaire entrepreneur with a thriving online business, an international speaker, and an inspiration to many.

Yet in 2017, I took an overdose and wanted to end it all.

Back then, if you had told me I would go from a suicidal deadbeat to an international speaker and a top affiliate for a huge software company within one year of trying to take my own life, I would have asked you what you were smoking. Heck, I would have asked you for some!

My aim for this book is to provide hope for those who feel hopeless, strength for those who feel weak, and inspiration for those who feel lost. Very few people know what it is like to be truly at rock bottom. When it takes hold of you, it is suffocating. It pins you down and makes you feel like you're never going to be able to get up and you shouldn't even try.

I don't want anyone else to ever feel like that again.

That's why I have made it my mission to share my story and inspire as many people as possible. I've been in the deepest reaches of depression and despair and managed to come out the other side. You can too.

This book will share my story toward rock bottom and then describe how I pulled myself up from a darkness few ever emerge from. It also chronicles my journey toward owning a seven-figure business, which held its own thorny and difficult challenges. Then, at the end of this book, I am going to share the method I used to achieve the life I have now.

If you are "in the suck" right now, I hope this book inspires you to make your own changes. It was designed to inspire, uplift, and motivate you to take action and keep going. If you do the best to better yourself, your life can look completely different in just a year's time.

For me, after trying and failing at lots of different things, I found something that suited my character and not only gave me the life and freedom I desired, but also changed the lives of my mum, my family, and tens of thousands of people around the world.

But if you had told me this as a child, I never would have believed you.

PART 1

THE PATH TO ROCK BOTTOM

CHAPTER 1

How It All Started

I struggle to remember a lot of my childhood. The remaining memories are patchy, and I struggle to attach emotions to them.

Guess that's a by-product of being numb for so long.

I lived with my grandparents for the first year of my life in a little town called King Lynn. When I was one, Mum got her own place about ten miles away from my grandparents. I was an only child up until the age of nine. Mum "joked" that having me put her off having any more kids ever again.

Grandad was my favorite person in the world, closely followed by Nan. Grandad spent a lot of time with me: we would sit on the wall outside the house, counting cars and guessing their makes and models. We would go for hikes in the woods or adventures through the sands of an old quarry turned national park. Grandad was an avid train enthusiast, and he had a massive electric railway in the garage we would often play with. Some of the fondest memories of my life are of spending time with him, walking through the woods, going into town, and playing with the trains. For a seventy-year-old man, Grandad was extremely fit. He would keep up with me all day long!

Nan didn't spend a whole lot of time with me; she was busy selling antiques most of the time. She showered me with gifts and bought me anything I wanted, regardless of my behavior. Mum tried to discipline me in her own way, but when Mum said no, Nan would say yes, and my mum was too dependent on my grandparents to push back.

My nan loved me, but she interfered too much in my life. It made me lose all respect for my mum and pretty much anyone and turned me into a spoiled brat.

Around the age of five is where things started going downhill.

My mother had very bad taste in men, and one of the first boyfriends I can remember was no exception. He was a violent lowlife who enjoyed hurting me. He would throw apples or other objects at me. He would restrain me for no reason and intentionally hurt me because it was funny. I was only five years old at this point and couldn't do anything back. When I tried, he would hurt me even more.

When you've had it easy your entire life and had everything handed to you on a silver platter, you turn soft. You're not able to deal with things as well as someone who was born into struggle. At just five years old, my life turned from heaven to hell pretty fast, and this was just the beginning.

My life went from getting whatever I wanted and having no consequences for my actions to being physically, emotionally, and verbally abused on a regular basis.

It was not all bad. My grandparents were still very active in my life, and I loved them more than anything. Grandad was especially involved and was the only person I could talk to and trust. He was a kind and wise man, the best man I've ever known.

Despite having loving grandparents and a mother who did her best with the darkening circumstances, I went into decline. My mother had been sheltered her whole life, and she felt like she had had no freedom until she was of age. She didn't want that for her children, so she interfered in my life as little as possible and pretty much left me to my own devices. Couple this with the fact that Nan bought me everything I wanted, and I turned into a spoiled brat who didn't respect anyone or anything. Combine *that* with being beaten and verbally abused by the father figures in my life, and I was set to turn into a very nasty person.

The year the original PlayStation came out, I destroyed three of them. I smashed them, stamped on them, and threw them at the wall.

Each time, my nan bought me another the next day.

It made me not respect or value anything. If I wanted something, I would do everything in my power to get it by any means necessary.

I was turning into a nasty, spoiled brat with no boundaries and no respect for anyone.

I didn't appreciate anything.

I had no morals, no respect, and no mercy.

The anger I felt toward the male role models in my life caused me to frequently explode on everyone around me. I hit other kids for very small reasons, and everyone moved out of the way for me in the school hallways. I once stabbed a kid in the back with a pen simply because he didn't agree with me. On the very first day of school, the teacher put her hand in front of me and I bit her. I was a violent lowlife, just like most of the male role models in my life.

I didn't have any respect for my mum and didn't do as I was told unless I was physically threatened. She once threw a chair across the room that bounced off the fire guard and hit me in the head. I was only eight years old.

At this time in my life, I started seeing a psychiatrist. I was prescribed sleeping tablets, labeled a problem child, and diagnosed with ADHD, which required even more pills every day to calm me down. Back then, they didn't have all the support and understanding they do today. You simply got labeled a problem child and were drugged up to the eyeballs.

There was a thick distrust between my mum and me. She wouldn't believe a word I said, even when I was telling the truth.

I turned into a horrible person, truly not caring about anyone or anything and doing things I am not proud of.

Yet this was a cakewalk compared to what happened next.

Not long after my ADHD diagnosis, my mum met another dysfunctional boyfriend. His solution to my misbehaving was to intimidate me and, when that didn't work, to beat me. We moved in with him after my mum had dated him for a while. He was a strange man, and most of the things he did made no sense to me. But he was the adult, so what he said went.

Looking back at it now, I see he was messed up in the head. He once took revenge on the neighbor's kids by peeing into a bucket and pouring it out a window over them when they walked down the side of the house. He filled up balloons with sugar water to get bees to sting the kids, too. When we first moved in, it was just me and him and my mum. It wasn't too bad at this point, but things soon got worse.

I remember my mum saying it was all my fault we moved in with him because I seemed to like him. My mum can't remember saying that, so I don't know if it was my own messed-up head that created that memory to make myself feel even worse or if it actually happened. She has blocked out many memories of her actions and experiences for fear of facing reality. I'm told I do the same: there have been many times in my life I have blocked out things I've done because the guilt and pain was too much to bear.

Back to the story at hand...

Mum's new boyfriend would beat me for trivial reasons, and I never knew when I was going to get it. The worst time was when

I accidentally clogged the toilet. I had blocked it once before, and he said if I did it again, he would beat the crap out of me.

Next time it clogged, I got a jug and tried to pour the contents out the window. But I spilled water on his precious magazines on the window ledge, and when he found out, he went ballistic. He dragged me up the stairs and proceeded to beat me for what seemed like an eternity. He threw me on the bed and suffocated me by holding a pillow over my face while I screamed and shouted, begging him to stop. I squirmed for minutes, telling him I couldn't breathe. His response was: "If you couldn't breathe, you wouldn't be making any noise." He beat and suffocated me with a duvet and pillow for what felt like hours. I was claustrophobic for years after that.

The beatings would usually end with me sobbing in my room. I still had no respect for anyone or anything, but if I acted up, I would get two tons of crap beat out of me.

I was a problem child, and I did things to annoy and upset everyone. My mum beat the crap out of me with a belt one day while her boyfriend and his daughter were both listening and laughing by the door.

I was turning into a very nasty person with no respect, no remorse, and no care for anyone or anything around me.

Still, I hadn't turned into a *completely* heartless prick just yet. My brother had just been born, and I resolved to stick up for him against my mother's dysfunctional boyfriend.

Once, the boyfriend shook my baby brother, and I remember scream-ing at him, "Get your fucking hands off my brother." He then turned his attention to me. The manhandling and abuse got worse after that. It got so bad that at night, I started to pee in the corner of my room instead of opening the bedroom door and risking an encounter.

Things weren't much better at school. I was still labeled a problem child, and because of all the issues at home, I found it hard to con-centrate. Some teachers were sympathetic and understanding, but others made it their mission to try and subdue me through humili-ation and intimidation.

One time, a teacher told me a wrong answer during a break and then called on me to answer the question during class. She had purposely fed me a load of crap to make me look like an idiot and proceeded to make me look stupid in front of the entire class. That stayed with me for years. I became more hesitant to answer questions and be outspoken due to the humiliations I suffered because of these teach-ers. Even when I knew the answer to something, I wouldn't speak up because of the embarrassment I had faced before.

It got so bad that if I ever spoke up about anything or was asked a question in class, I would go bright red, my heart would race, and I would feel hot, like I was going to pass out.

It took a lot of work, but now I realize it doesn't matter if you're right or wrong. You've got to take the leap. The reason I have progressed so far in the last five years is because I went for it with everything I had and pushed through my fears of being wrong and making a fool of myself. When I slipped up, I reminded myself I was at least trying. When I embarrassed myself or felt stupid, I learned to shrug the anxiety off, knowing it would pass. I learned the more I did something, the easier it became, and acting fast meant more opportunities to become great, which built my confidence.

But at this time, I was still a screwed-up kid being imprinted with the screwed-up lessons that would follow me throughout life until I reinvented myself.

Throughout this entire time, I never really had any friends. I had some people who pretended to be my friends for a bit, but they weren't true friends. I felt alone for a long time, and it messed me up and continued to make me a bad person.

One day, after one of the worst beatings and with massive bruises on my shoulders, I had enough. At school, every time I saw a teacher, I would pull my sleeve aside to display my bruises until the teachers asked how I got them, and then I sang like a canary.

Social services got involved and gave my mum a choice: her kids or her partner.

It didn't take her long to dump the man and pack her bags.

We were about to move again to a brand-new place in a brand-new area where I knew no one. A "fresh start" where my mother, brother, and I could start again.

It was supposed to be a new beginning, but things were about to get a lot worse.

CHAPTER 2

Toward Rock Bottom

After escaping my mother's most recent boyfriend and the abuse that came from him, this new place was meant to be a fresh start. But I would have taken any day of my former life over what came next.

Our fresh little slice of hell was out in the middle of nowhere, a secluded ex-farm in the region of Sutton Bridge. I guess my mum thought moving away from civilization would give her more freedom. We were still only a forty-minute car ride from my grandparents, but we visited them less frequently.

This place was one of the worst. We had one neighbor who hated us, and we were miles from the nearest village. There was no escape or help to save me when things kicked off.

At this house, so many terrible things happened, it's hard to put them into a timeline.

Living with the previous man had turned my mum into a hoarder. The house was a mess, and our living standards began to sink. One day,

I jumped over a trash bag with bare feet and sliced the tip of my toe off on a tin can. This wasn't a measly cut; it went straight through the bone. My toe was held on by a thin piece of skin. The first thing out of my mum's mouth was, "You better not bleed on my new fucking carpet." To be fair to her, she didn't know how bad it was, and when she saw it, she took me to the hospital to get it stitched back on.

My mum would often leave us alone and hired a babysitter to take care of us. One day, the babysitter asked her brother to take over because she was too busy.

This guy was one of the sickest, most twisted people I would ever meet.

February 23, 2000, is a date I will never forget. It was this day I was molested for the first time. Sadly, it was far from the last time. It was a day that broke me completely. The day that started me on a downward spiral that almost killed me.

When something like this happens to you, it's like a part of you has been taken that you can never get back. It's like losing all your self-worth, dignity, and self-respect at once. It's like being at the bottom of the barrel where no one cares at all. It's like nothing matters anymore.

I couldn't tell anyone—I couldn't even admit it to myself.

The sick bastard would get a kick out of watching the movie *Titanic* while he abused me. To this day, I can't watch that movie; the song sends shivers down my spine.

He abused me for months, and it changed me forever. Once a relatively outspoken, boisterous child, I shrank to a subdued, fearful shadow of my former self with a rage that would give Bruce Banner a run for his money.

One day, the babysitter's brother was chasing me around the garden with an air rifle. He aimed it at me over the hood of my mum's car and pointed it right at my face. He pulled the trigger at point-blank range, and I felt one of the worst pains I have ever felt in my life just below my eye.

I was completely blind in my right eye. He had hit me on the bone just below my right eye socket. I was screaming, rolling on the ground, and certain I would never see properly again. It stung worse than anything I had ever experienced. I howled like a banshee for an hour, the fact that I still couldn't see anything stoking the panic and anguish.

It was a good five hours before I started to regain my vision.

This was just one of the many sick and twisted things he did to hurt me over the months. He tortured me in ways I don't want to remember.

This went on for a while until all of it came out. My mum was fuming. It turned out he had allegedly abused over twenty other kids in the town as well but had never been caught. As I understand it, most victims got bricks through their windows and other intimidatory threats to make them keep their mouths shut. The rest were too young to testify. I was told he got a cushy witness protection program down in London and a new name to boot.

Video games were an escape for me, and I spent a lot of time on my beloved PlayStation.

Once, at my grandparents' place, I was playing on my computer in their living room and heard someone screaming for help from upstairs. I rushed through the house to see Nan on the floor, clutching her chest. Grandad and Mum were at the other end of the house and could not hear her.

I ran downstairs as fast as I could to alert them, and my nan was rushed to the hospital. Thankfully, she survived: the hospital said she was found just in time. I remember feeling so happy I had saved my nan's life.

Yet that happiness, like every happiness back then, was short-lived, as I returned to hell later that day.

I went to a number of different schools while we lived in Sutton Bridge. I missed about a year of school too. We had a new head teacher at one of the schools, and he was used to the days of corporal punishment and showed it. After he assaulted me, I refused to go back. Of course, I couldn't prove it, so after refusing to go to school for over six months, I changed schools.

After the latest troubles in school, I lost what little respect I had for my mum. We hated each other. Physical threats were the only way she could control me. But at this time, I was getting to be bigger and started overpowering my mum in our physical confrontations.

It was a truly horrible time.

My mum had a breakdown, swearing she was going to kill herself. She started burning everything she owned and said she was going to jump in it afterward. You *never* want to see your mum that way, even if you are an emotionally challenged brat who supposedly has no respect for anyone and doesn't care about anything.

It was around this time child services got involved and my mum put me into care. I had lost all respect for my mother and had barely a care for anyone else's thoughts, feelings, or emotions.

In my eyes, my brother was the reason I was being taken away from my mother. This was further stoked by my mum's exact words: "It's not safe for you to be here with your brother." This built up a lot of hatred and resentment over the years, which made a big show of itself later on.

I went into foster care with a few other kids and a couple.

I really should have stayed there.

The couple was very strict, and I was terrified of the guy. He never hurt us, but the way he spoke and shouted instilled fear in all of us. It was just what I needed to go from a disrespectful little brat with no boundaries to someone who actually cared about something. But I didn't stay long enough to change for the better.

I spoke to my mum on the phone and cried to her almost every night because of how much I hated having to do as I was told.

A month later, she pulled me out, and I was home again.

We went back into the exact same circle. I acted out, and Mum struggled with discipline and putting her foot down. In less than two weeks, we were at each other's throats again and a breakdown was imminent.

That was when I was taken into care again, this time with two ladies.

Although nothing terrible happened while I was with them, I hated every minute of it. They were strict as hell and were definitely not people I could open up to. As always, I was alone. The only person I could confide in and talk to was myself.

I visited my nan and gradad every so often, but I never talked about how I felt. I always kept everything to myself.

Telling people how I felt was a sign of weakness in my eyes, and I had been ridiculed for it in the past. Every time I got excited about something, I was told to calm down, to shut up, or that I was stupid. "Don't big yourself up, because it ain't pretty," I was told. That stuck with me until a few short years ago.

It was at this time I went from a child who didn't give a damn about anything or anyone to the complete opposite. All my mistakes had long-lasting, mortifying consequences, and instead of being carefree and unfiltered, I started becoming scared to make a wrong move. I started to withdraw and overthink before I did anything.

The months blurred together, and I can't remember much about this time. I just remember how it ended.

After feeling scared and suppressed by these two women for so long, I snapped. I told one of them, "I don't give a fuck," and started throwing her ornaments around. When her partner, the more stern and scary of the two, came back, I did the same thing.

My rage, loneliness, and messed-up brain outweighed the fear I had of these two women, and I screamed, shouted, cried, and floundered into a cornucopia of emotions for hours until I was too exhausted to move.

Later that week, I was moved to another foster home.

Old Leake was one of the best places I have ever lived. I truly wish I had stayed there. It was a farm where I learned how to work and how to enjoy it. I mucked out stables, shot shotguns, rode horses and dirt bikes, and felt I could really talk to the couple I lived with.

I had a few outbursts and some things happened, but most of it was instigated by their real son, who did not want me around. He would set me up, annoy me, and encourage me to act out so I would get into trouble. Of course, their son was the one they believed when anything happened. And he would lie his ass off to get me in trouble so he could have his parents back to himself again.

It was while I was staying here that my nan passed away. I wasn't even allowed to go to the funeral to say goodbye. My nan interfered too much, but she loved me. Along with my grandad, she was the person I loved most in the world.

At this home, I remember going to a new school and lasting three days. By this time in my life, I was trying to control my anger and make an effort. But there was one child in that school who thought he could bully me. He was two years older than me, and after three days of pinching me, punching me, pulling my hair, and winding me up every chance he got, I snapped. I rammed him up against the wall by his throat and choked him until staff members arrived. I was still screaming in a fit of rage, writhing while five fully grown adults held me down, when my foster parents came to the school almost an hour later.

Even despite that, I mostly enjoyed my time at the farm, and if I had stayed there, maybe things would not have continued to worsen.

Eventually, they got rid of me. The final straw was when I grabbed their son by the collar and ripped one of his buttons on his new shirt. As usual, he had provoked me, and I saw his eyes light up when it happened as he rushed off to get me into trouble one last time.

After that, I didn't get the luxury of foster care anymore.

I went into children's homes, where the real messed-up kids go.

There, I discovered yet another level of hell.

I really started to decline in the children's homes. I was moved on a regular basis, spending one- to six-month stints in various hellholes around the country, never getting to know anyone, trusting the wrong people, getting betrayed, and generally becoming a shell of a human.

The first children's home was by far the worst. The children were horrible. The staff were just as bad. This was where I started losing a lot more confidence and was bullied and intimidated on a daily basis by those older, stronger, and bigger than me. I was barely thirteen years old, and many of the older children were turning seventeen.

The staff weren't much better. Many of them assaulted me. I got dragged up stairs by my feet, had my head smashed on car trunks, and was slammed against cabinets inside the rooms. The place was out of control, and when certain combinations of staff members were on duty together, it was a hellish time. We kids gave as good as we got, verbally and physically abusing the staff right back.

It was a fucked-up playground of suffering. Of course, the few staff members who were half-decent never believed us. And the rotten ones knew where all the cameras were so they never got caught.

The children weren't much better. Some of them tortured and killed small animals and smashed their carcasses all over the walls for fun. Others were just plain enthused by suffering and made it their mission to make everyone's lives miserable.

That place was horrible. I went from someone who was clearly having issues and breaking down to someone who was downright out of his mind.

The months have blurred into one as I've tried to forget that place over the years, but I remember two specific incidents clearly.

One time, I threw my boots at the back of one of the staff's cars, and he grabbed my head, rammed it onto the car hood, and lectured me about respect. He pinned me there for a few minutes until I stopped squirming.

Another time, I had barricaded myself in my room and the deputy manager, one of the worst of them all, smashed his way through the door.

He destroyed some drawers and other furniture I had stacked against the door as he forced his way in. He subsequently grabbed my head and rammed it into the broken drawers before anyone else could see what was happening and blamed me for standing close to the door. He told the others the violence had happened upon entry and it was unavoidable.

I finally got moved from there sometime later, and the place got shut down not long afterward. I have no idea what happened to the demons that lived and worked there. I just hope the staff were prosecuted and they didn't end up torturing some other poor children at another home.

While I was being pushed from pillar to post, my mum got another boyfriend, Jonathan, and then my youngest brother was born.

Out of all of my mum's boyfriends, Jonathan was one of the best. He never got physical. He was an English teacher and just made me feel bad with his words instead.

He hated me and I hated him, but at this point in my life, I hated anyone who said something I didn't want to hear.

The next place, Albion Street, was not too bad on the grand scale of things. Some of the kids were bullies who hit me sometimes. One humiliating experience stands out in particular: to this day, I'm very nervous around women because of a few painful experiences with girls, and this was one of the first.

We were all out in town. There were about twenty of us, and a girl said, "Close your eyes and I'll kiss you." Instead of kissing me, she slapped me round the face as hard as she could—in front of everyone. It was planned.

That was one of the most embarrassing moments of my life. I had already suffered from girls tormenting me in the past, and this only stoked that inferno of doubt around women.

Throughout my years of being put down, humiliated, abused, and beaten by both peers and authority figures, I began to go numb. I moved so often and was so worried about what other people thought of me that I didn't know how to act. I was never myself. I lost myself, and sometimes I wonder if I was *ever* myself during those years. I developed a chameleonlike reflex where I would blend into my new surroundings by becoming a drone, never having an original thought, agreeing to everything.

I acted like I was normal and fit in everywhere, but on the inside, I was dying. When you suppress yourself for that long, you can never be yourself around anyone, never trust anyone, and feel so completely isolated that you think you can never come back.

It was suffocating, unending darkness, and the only way to escape it was to disconnect from reality and become a yes-man, nodding and agreeing and never having an original thought or reaction.

On the outside, I looked fine. I molded myself to those around me and was different depending on who I was hanging out with.

No one knew I was dying and losing my entire identity on the inside.

One day, I climbed into one of the top windows above the stairs and threatened to jump out of it, saying I wanted to kill myself. I don't think I did actually want to; I think I wanted attention more than anything.

Regardless, that stunt landed me in a secure unit.

That place was hell, too. It was a mental hospital with some very strange people.

One guy never said a word. He would just walk up to people and punch them in the face.

Another girl was completely messed up—couldn't speak or anything—and just played on the swing the entire day.

There was a padded room with plastic windows they would lock you in if you so much as raised your voice to someone. I lost count of how many times I was thrown in that room in the short time I was there.

The whole place had the feel of a hospital, with a big plastic window in the office so the staff could keep an eye on everyone. There was a school on-site, and we were allowed very little freedom.

I saw a psychiatrist every day and talked about why I had threatened to jump from the window. I begged to leave and told the staff I was just kidding around.

They weren't having any of it.

I was there for thirty days, or maybe it was sixty. I remember requesting to be moved back a few times and being denied.

My heart sank each day I stayed there, and I cried myself to sleep almost every single night.

When I eventually was allowed to leave, I went back to Albion Street.

Although I was only fourteen, they gave me back an extremely dry packet of tobacco they had confiscated from me when I first arrived. The first thing I did when I walked out of that door was roll a harsh, dry cigarette from that dusty packet. I didn't care. It was nicotine, and I needed it.

I never threatened to kill myself again after that.

Throughout all this, I never had any heart-to-heart talks with anyone. I had surface-level conversations. I trusted no one except my grandad, and I still didn't even feel I could talk to him about everything.

It was around this time that he passed away.

I was devastated. It was the most painful thing I had ever felt.

Grandad was the only one I ever talked to. He was the only person in my screwed-up reality I trusted. The only one to never let me down —and now he was gone.

Now I was truly alone.

I attended his funeral. I was absolutely adamant that I was going to be there for his funeral. Although I was extremely upset, I still couldn't cry at it.

I never cried in front of anyone, but during the alone times, I cried into my pillow, sounding like a wounded banshee. It was common for me to cry every day, multiple times a day.

I had always been quite isolated, but this was when I started shutting myself away from the world completely.

Less than two weeks after my grandad passed, I had my grammar school test. It was a test of ability, and those who passed would go to a prestigious grammar school for gifted students.

I always got high marks on everything I tried. During my school years, I would often finish tests in half the time of everyone else and then be told to sit and wait while the other kids finished. I wasn't having any of it. I would act out. A kid with no respect and ADHD sitting in boredom when he aced a test twice as fast as everyone else? Yeah, that wasn't gonna happen.

On the test, I was just three points shy of being accepted into a grammar school. I couldn't concentrate; I had been in a permanent state of misery since my grandad passed. The only good thing in my life had been ripped away and they wanted me to sit a test to secure my place in a school I didn't give two craps about at the time, so I was not on top of my game.

I felt like I was truly alone, destined to suffer.

I endured this torture day in and day out.

I created a cover. I looked good on the outside but on the inside I was eating my heart out. I developed canned responses, said the same thing in situations all the time to avoid conflict, and always stuck to what was safe and familiar. If it worked in a social situation before, it must be okay, right? Doing that for so long took away all of my creativity and free thinking and turned me into a robot that was too scared to have an original thought.

The problems in school continued. I went to a few different schools while at Albion Street and never lasted more than a month at each. I had home tutoring, which entailed a tutor coming to watch me play video games and explain how they were teaching me more than school ever could. Albion Street didn't like that and told me I would have to move to a place with a school on-site.

My social worker told me we were going to go to McDonald's to discuss it, but she lied. As soon as I got in the car, the doors were bolted and I was shipped to my next dose of hell in another terrible children's home.

This was my final children's home.

I think I was there for almost two years, and it was horrible. Unlike Albion Street, they were strict on no smoking, and I was addicted. Kids came and went while I was there, but a few were constant. As usual, they pretended to be my friends when it suited them but mainly used me for their own desires.

One kid in particular got moved because it was dangerous for him to stay there after how many children he had taunted. One day, I looked up to see him standing at the top of the stairs while I was in the living room. He shouted down, "Go fuck your dead grandad." I felt a blood-red rage sweep over me. Before he finished the sentence, I bolted after him up the stairs, but he managed to get to his room and lock the door. I hammered on it for over an hour. The bottom of the solid metal door was slightly bent when I finished.

The staff stood near me but didn't intervene. They were wary of what would happen if I did get in. I'm very glad he managed to get away, because I think I would have killed him.

The big bully of the place was the next door over, and he came out and told me, "Shut the fuck up." I glared at him and told him to fuck off. He stared at me but didn't do anything because the staff were watching. This guy was a major bully and much older and stronger than me as a fourteen-year-old kid. One time, as we were waiting in the car, he grabbed my wrist and dug his nail into my skin for an entire minute, not letting go as I screamed. He went so deep with his nail, I still have the scar today.

Another guy who I thought was my friend just used me. Once I moved, I called him and he said, "Stop calling me, you fat, freaky, fucking weirdo," and hung up.

I still didn't have much discipline, and some of the adults made a point of annoying me to get a reaction out of me and get me into trouble. I hated most of the teachers and a lot of the staff.

Some of the punishments were cruel and unusual, the biggest of which was them stopping me from having my teeth fixed. I was supposed to have four teeth removed and braces to correct my smile and was put on a waiting list. I had always had bad teeth and was very self-conscious about them. When the time came, they rejected the treatment because of my behavior, and they never got done. It's why I have braces today and am only now getting my mouth sorted out at the age of thirty-two.

Staff would often refuse to take me places as punishment—or just because they didn't want to. Once, they took a group of us to a youth club. When we arrived, we realized the time was wrong and we were an hour early and had to go back. While we were driving, Chay, the guy who I kicked the door in on, annoyed the crap out of me, and I threatened him with a lighter. Lighters weren't allowed, and I knew I had just lost my ride back to the youth club. So I opened the car door and told the driver to stop. He slowed to around thirty miles per hour but refused to stop.

Youth club was a nice escape for me and I really liked one of the girls there, and I wasn't about to walk three hours from the children's home to come back later.

So I jumped and rolled onto the road.

I don't know how I managed to roll and not smash my face on the concrete.

Apart from a few cuts and bruises, I was fine. I stood up and they just drove off without so much as stopping to see if I was all right.

There were a few things to be happy about in that place. We had our own psychiatric doctor on-site at this home. He was a nice Chinese man who always let us choose an herbal Chinese tea whenever we went to see him, which was mandated each week by the care home. And one teacher, Joe, was my favorite guy in the whole place. He was a kind soul who listened and never acted on impulse. He tried to understand us instead of controlling us. He was always on my side in the team meetings.

When the children's home finally kicked me out for refusing to stop smoking, he was in my corner, protesting, "There are much bigger issues with James than his smoking; you are just trying to get rid of him." I will always be grateful to him for trying.

It didn't work, though, and the children's home expelled me. I had broken my collarbone while fighting with one of the kids there; it was rebroken by one of the staff when they manhandled me to make me leave the school grounds.

At this point, I was fifteen years old.

CHAPTER 3

Hitting Rock Bottom

During this time, I was totally alone. I couldn't speak to my mum about anything, the counselor didn't help, and I trusted absolutely no one. Such profound loneliness is a horrendous feeling. It makes you feel like you shouldn't even try and there is no point in living. It feels impossible to fall any further, like this is as bad as it gets.

If only I knew the place below the bottom.

When the children's home threw me out, I ended up moving back in with my mum. It was a few months before I turned sixteen. This was the worst possible time for a move because if I had left the care system after I turned sixteen, child services would have supported me until I was twenty-one. Yet I came out a few months before and ended up with no support at all.

Things were good for a month or so, but it didn't take long before I started pushing boundaries again due to my mum's lack of discipline. At this point in my life, I was not a very nice person. All the crap I had endured had turned me into an aggressive person, reenacting the hurt

I had endured by inflicting it on others around me. My brothers got the worst of it. I was jealous and resentful that they had spent their entire lives with my mum and had easy, cushy upbringings with no discipline. I especially blamed my middle brother, since my behavior around him was part of why I'd been put into care in the first place.

He hadn't done anything to get me sent away. I was the problem, and it wasn't safe for me to be around my brother when he was younger because of my rage and outbursts. But I never took the blame for anything at this point in my life. I shoved it onto others and refused to accept any responsibility, therefore rendering myself incapable of any change.

My mum had another boyfriend by now. He rarely raised a hand against us, but he did one day when he grabbed me by the throat and rammed me up against a car because I got in his face. He constantly made me feel worthless and obviously favored my brothers more than me. I found out much later that he was just as bad as all the others, if not worse.

I was a social outcast by this point. Having lived in children's homes with strange people with strange habits, I had no clue how a normal person was supposed to behave. I made two friends through a babysitter my mum hired for my brothers. But they weren't real friends; they just used me. We used to hang out and have fun, but in the end, they just used me to get what they wanted.

On my sixteenth birthday, we moved again. I spent my sixteenth birthday packing boxes and loading up a van.

This time we didn't move very far, just to a fixer-upper a couple of villages away. I still kept in contact with my "friends" until we got drunk one time and I told them they were taking the piss. The next time I spoke to them, they invited me to the village, so I hopped on my bike to apologize. When I got off my bike, a giant guy who must have been three times my size emerged. He started punching me and told me if I came anywhere near there again, I would get it even worse. I went home crying and again had no friends and no one to talk to.

By this point, I was already heavily into video games. After losing my friends, I played even more. All I did was get up and play video games. I was getting false senses of accomplishment from them. Getting lost in another reality and forgetting about the real world was the only way I stayed sane and happy.

I had no common sense, and one day I was playing with a steamer, not realizing the damage one could do with it. I burned my brother with it so badly, I had to stay on my own in the house for months while the trial went on.

At this time, I lived off microwaved baked potatoes.

I was playing games more than ever. I once spent an entire weekend, Friday to Monday, on an online game without sleep.

I was a mess.

When the trial was over, I was ordered to leave home. I wasn't allowed to stay with my mum and brothers anymore. I went into a kind of care home with mostly people aged forty and above. It was strange: I was the youngest one there, and most of the dysfunctional adults were very strange. I hated it and tried to show my face as little as possible.

I went to college for a while while I was there, but never really made any good friends. I was too nervous all the time. I could barely say anything except the same generic crap I said to everyone.

After a few altercations in this new care home, I left.

I stayed on my mum's couch for a few weeks before I found a place in the Foyer, a group house for people my age. It was a pretty good place; it had some ups and downs, but for the most part it wasn't too bad.

Following a series of unfortunate events in one of the worst colleges in the country, I dropped out a few months into the program.

When I started on the course there were more than twenty of us. By the time I left there were only around seven remaining.

I started a new training course and after a few months found a girlfriend.

My first proper girlfriend, at the age of seventeen.

For the first time, I felt like I had someone to talk to. I didn't tell her everything. I was ashamed of my past, but it was nice to have someone to try to open up to. Unfortunately, she had her own issues and was constantly in trouble with the police. I got dragged into it sometimes, and after a while, I got kicked out of the Foyer.

I had been given chance after chance because the staff saw something in me. I did as much as three other people who got kicked out separately, and they still didn't kick me out. The final straw was when my girlfriend said she wanted to enroll in the army. I was devastated. I cried, and as soon as I got back to the Foyer, I smashed every single thing in my room, ripped the lights from the ceiling, and caused a power cut. I caused over £1,000 worth of damage during that hissy fit, and then I was out on my own again. She didn't end up going into the army after all, and I messed up for no reason at all.

I found a flat my mum's friends had just moved out of. It was a wreck: the landlord didn't do anything, and it was moldy, decrepit, and in disrepair. But it was a roof. I moved in the day I moved out of the Foyer, and this was where I started getting involved with the wrong people.

I was constantly drunk or on something. My girlfriend and I spent all our time drinking and making mischief. A few months later, we broke up.

I had been insecure about the relationship and wanted to see how long she would go without calling me if I didn't call her, since I always called her. Apparently, she had heard a nasty rumor about me, and when we finally connected again after a week of no talking, she asked me about it.

"I can't believe you would even think that of me," I replied instantly in a text message. "We're done."

It was Christmas Eve, and I instantly regretted sending that in a rush and a rage. But it was done.

The next few weeks were some of the most tormented and twisted weeks of my life. I constantly cried; I was under the influence of something all the time. I couldn't drink enough: every day, I tried to numb the pain until I passed out. The fact that I had said that to her and messed everything up tortured my mind, and there was nothing I could do.

The only person I could talk to and the only person I loved at the time was gone, and it was my fault.

I slid further into depression and anxiety. I was scared to breathe. My actions had had such negative and permanent consequences that I was scared to do anything anymore.

It was at this point I lost what small part of my individuality was remaining. I became a mindless zombie around new people. Saying the same old generic crap in conversation. Never so much as venturing a word off my script for fear of the consequences. I completely shut off all emotions as much as possible, and fits of stifled rage would boil to the surface when it all got too much.

I got a reputation for being a pushover: in the world I was involved in, that was a big no-no.

I got robbed regularly. I got robbed at knifepoint, machete-point, axe-point, and even gunpoint. I had people come through my windows with baseball bats. I was getting more and more broken, and more and more with the wrong crowd.

Why didn't I just up and leave?

It was a vicious feedback loop. I would just about to get on my feet, and then I would get screwed over. I guess I wanted to prove I could make it where I was. I just didn't realize how much damage it was doing to stay there.

I had so much pent-up rage from all the abuse and circumstances that I constantly lashed out. My best friend once hit me on the head with a padlock. Believe it or not, it was a genuine accident, but I launched myself on him and almost gouged his eyes out. I broke so many Xbox controllers, the Tesco staff asked me why I was buying so many and thought I was reselling them.

In the end, lashing out at others got me into too much trouble, and breaking things became too costly.

So I took my anger out on myself, frequently punching myself in the head, headbutting walls, and cutting myself. I've had so many blows to the head, I am genuinely surprised I don't have brain damage.

All the times I had lashed out and raged before this were cries for help. If someone had actually reached out and talked to me, it might have made a difference, but no one did.

If someone had taken the time to speak to me and understand what I was going through, I may have not sunk so low. If we can understand why people are acting the way they are instead of judging them and reacting to them, maybe we can help them instead of throwing them under the bus.

Around this time, my mum lived fifteen miles away. I once went bowling with her neighbor's son and ran into an old friend. Seeing her was a shock: this friend was the reason my first girlfriend and I had broken up. According to her, her boyfriend had made up a rumor that I had raped her, and my first girlfriend had heard about it.

It was absolutely heart-wrenching to hear that rumor attached to my name. And then to hear it from the girl you love and to know it's messing with her head? That messed me up badly.

I ended up walking home with this friend and her boyfriend. As we crossed over a bridge, I asked her who started that vicious rumor. She told me it was the very boyfriend we were walking with at that moment. I'll be honest: I contemplated killing him and throwing him off the bridge, but I was so run-down and broken that I couldn't even muster the courage to confront him.

I was a pussy.

A wannabe pussy in a world I didn't belong in.

Looking back at it, I am not so sure it was him; she was probably making the whole thing up to see if I would attack him. He could have been in the same boat as me, being used and abused by her until she decided she was done with him.

I genuinely think if you falsely say another human being committed a crime, you should be sentenced to that crime's punishment. The damage that accusatory lies can do to someone's image, mental health, and life can be irreversible.

For me, it still shows up today. I still struggle to make a move on women. I am so absolutely terrified of rejection or of something being misconstrued, it's taken me years to be able to function around other women. I am better now but still very wary and nervous—and that stems from the incidents I had with other girls growing up.

I felt very lost and alone, but this was nothing I wasn't used to.

Every day was the same thing.

Wake up, drink and smoke myself into oblivion, play video games, pass out.

This went on for a while until a youth team I had been assigned to suggested I do something to get out of the house. I volunteered in the British Heart Foundation to try and improve my social skills. I could never get a job or hold one for very long, so this was my way of not being a full hermit.

I met a girl there who, like me, rented a dump of a place. We found a rental house and lived together for a while as friends. It was such a relief to be at a house that didn't have the imminent feeling of danger all the time.

The house we moved into was still less than adequate, so the council moved us to a brand-new council house. The girl offered to sort out the financial particulars, which was nice of her—or so I thought. I still didn't do much but play video games at this point. I was losing myself in a virtual world to escape reality most days.

A few months into the new lease, I called up because of a problem with the house. I spoke to someone from the council, but they would not talk to me because I was not a tenant, apparently. I said I was a joint tenant, and they told me no: I was merely a lodger, so I had no control or rights at all.

Not only that, I found out she was lying about the rent too! She had been overcharging me for my half and pocketing the rest.

So I had no rights to the brand-new council house we had just been awarded. I wasn't one to keep quiet in these matters, so soon after that, a confrontation ensued, and I moved out.

After this final kick to the balls, betrayed trust, and meeting some of the most twisted people on the planet...

I was done.

I went full hermit.

I gave up.

Video games were my reality now.

I was an anxious, shy, withdrawn, depressed individual.

I was always on something to keep my anxiety at bay.

I tried so many different antidepressants and antipsychotics.

Some would work for a while, and I would start to feel better and venture out into the world. Yet as sure as day, the world would beat me back into submission and they would stop working. Food, drugs, and alcohol became my go-to numbing agents.

I found it hard enough to be around new people, and locking myself away from the world with little to no social interactions only fanned those flames. My social anxiety went into overdrive, and I would use drink and drugs whenever I needed to be around other people. The only time I felt comfortable around others was when I was very drunk or on drugs.

I was always on something to numb the pain and try to fit in, and I was losing what little bit of my identity I had left.

I would say these years of seclusion and narcotically fuelled existence were the worst of my life, but sadly, with everything else I had endured over the years, that was not true.

These late teenage years, like so many others, blur into one, and I can only remember pieces. During this time, I lost my driver's license. This was a real harsh blow, as I lost all my freedom with it. I didn't feel safe walking down the street and was always on edge around other people. Driving had been one of the only times I felt truly protected.

I was on and off with a new girl who was even more messed up than I was, and that relationship ended in utter disaster.

Not long after, in an alcohol-induced rage, I exploded at my mum, with whom I had been living again, and trashed her house. After the fit, I had to move back out on my own.

Every day was the same ritual. Wake up, do whatever I could to not be alone with my thoughts and shut off the negativity and horror inside my own head, pass out, and repeat.

In a sick way, it worked: I shut myself down for so long, I began to feel nothing at all.

I kept repeating conversations I had heard, never having an original thought, and regurgitating the same sentences over and over because they were "safe."

As the years went on, I became a functional alcoholic. I would drink and take drugs all day and go along as normal to keep my anxiety in check.

After a few years of locking myself away, my best friend at the time tried to get me out into the real world. My friend set me up with a girl and we met at a bar. Drinking used to be a way for me to overcome my fears and relax, but even that didn't work anymore. Even after quite a few drinks, I literally couldn't bring myself to touch her. My anxiety and past experiences were inhibiting me from just picking my arm up and putting it on her shoulder. My friend had to pick my arm up and move it for me. I couldn't make a move by myself. It was terrible: I knew she liked me, but I just couldn't pick my arm up. I was broken.

I hadn't interacted with a woman for almost three years by this point.

This was early 2016.

My only remaining friend and I fell out a few months later due to me doing something I am not proud of while being under the influence. I was a jealous, bitter person, and my own stupidity made me lose the last friend I had.

And I was alone again.

I got worse before finally snapping at the beginning of 2017.

All I did was play video games. I got my false sense of accomplishments from them: being the best at games and building empires on them made me feel good. I still believe that without video games, I wouldn't be here, so I can't condemn them. Without relying on them for so many years, I definitely wouldn't be here now. They were a vice, but they saw me through the darkness.

Unfortunately, those feelings of accomplishment were getting shorter and shorter lived. I had completed so many games and had so many thousands of achievements, they didn't have the same effect. I was gaining a lot of weight from just sitting and playing video games all day, and my health started to severely deteriorate.

I was in decline.

In January 2017, I hit my lowest point.

They say that sometimes, you have to hit your lowest to be able to climb back up.

PART 2

CLIMBING MY WAY OUT

CHAPTER 4

Realization and Redemption

In January 2017, I took an overdose and thought my life was over.

I woke up two days later covered in my own vomit.

No one had found me.

The only person who cared about me was my mum, and she had been battling sepsis and diabetic neuropathy, so she couldn't come to check on me. I was alone, but I was used to that at this point.

I felt like shit, I looked like shit, and I smelled like shit. I got up, staggered to the kitchen, and tried to eat a Pot Noodle. It came back up within seconds. I slowly managed to keep some bread down before collapsing in my chair.

I was so run-down, I didn't even want to play video games. I didn't want to do anything at all.

I curled up and started watching *Game of Thrones* for the first time. The next few days passed by in a blur. I ate and watched *Game of Thrones*, barely able to move because of how run-down I was.

It was during this haze that something inside me snapped.

For the first time in a long time, I started to ask myself questions:

What are you doing?

Do you really want to go out like this?

Do you really want to leave your mum with a dead son?

Do you really want to end your life knowing you could have done so much and been someone?

No, I realized. The answer was a resounding *no*.

For so many years, I had just been existing and going along with everything, never taking a moment to talk to myself, never questioning why I was the way I was, always pushing everything down to hide from the world.

But if we ever want to become our best selves and live our best lives, then one day we all have to face ourselves and ask those difficult questions.

Once I started asking myself these difficult questions and becoming more self-aware, I started having epiphanies that shook me to the core.

The first one came almost instantaneously, right there in that chair, lighting the fire under my ass that would carry me to success:

One day, you're gonna feel like crap all the time. One day, you're gonna have no energy—you're gonna be old and unable to enjoy life...

It was like someone screaming at me inside my head...

So get off your ass and do something with your life.

At that moment, something changed.

It changed me and made me want to try again. It was like a switch being turned on after being off for so long. I had reached my very lowest point, the lowest I would allow myself to go before waking up and doing something about my sorry state.

Everyone has their low place, the place that is the lowest they will allow themselves to go before they start to do something about it. You may be coasting along in a job you hate, just getting by and being able to cope, when *boom*—you're laid off with negative $5,000 in the bank. That's your low point, after which you start becoming obsessed with changing your situation.

Maybe it is being fired, losing a loved one, falling into depression, getting dumped, becoming homeless.

For me, it was attempted suicide.

Whatever that point is for you, when you reach it (and you will know when you have reached it) is when you begin to climb.

There are countless success stories from people who fell all the way to the bottom and made huge steps forward after years of barely existing.

I realized something that fateful day: I had been wasting my limited time.

For years, I did nothing. I smoked, drank, and pissed my life away. I hid away from life, too scared to speak up, too terrified to go for what I wanted. I beat myself up and wallowed in self-pity. I was resigned to the knowledge that life had dealt me a bad hand and I had wasted all my opportunities.

I'm not alone. So many people in life settle for less than they can achieve. Meandering through life like zombies, never stretching themselves, never bettering themselves, giving up on their hopes and dreams.

But when you realize the fragility of life and that in the end your fears and embarrassments mean nothing, you can start truly living.

There are thousands of people every day who learn they're going to die in a month, or two months, or six months. And the sad thing is that for many, that moment is when they actually start to live. Fear goes away: they start to take action, take risks, and take chances.

That girl or guy they wanted to ask out but were too afraid of?

That place they wanted to travel to? That old friend they haven't seen in a while?

Suddenly, the fear and hesitation go away and they go for it.

They no longer procrastinate. They no longer hesitate.

And when you have been close to death and wasted so many years of your life on *nothing*, you realize there is only one guarantee in life: you are going to die.

That's it.

That is the only guarantee I or anyone else can give you. No one gets out of this alive.

If you knew you were going to die next week, what would you do differently? I guarantee you, you wouldn't be scared of pressing some buttons and making some mistakes. Fear and embarrassment are temporary. Regret lasts a lifetime.

Treat every day as if it were your last. Don't procrastinate and say, "I can do that tomorrow or next year." Because tomorrow never comes, and next year isn't guaranteed to us at all.

That fateful day, something awoke in me: a burning desire to make something of myself and make up for all the years I had wasted. For so many years, I had ignored my talents and my abilities and didn't even try to succeed at anything. Everyone else thought I was useless, that I would never amount to anything.

Everyone except one person.

My mum.

Despite our checkered past, my mum had always believed in me and knew I had great potential. But I had never believed *her*.

That needed to change. I needed to prove to everyone around me and myself that I wasn't some layabout loser, destined to fail. I was destined for so much more. I wanted to prove to myself that I could stand on my own two feet, that I could support myself, and that I was more than the broken shell of a human I had deteriorated into the last few years.

Around this time, I stopped smoking.

This was a massive challenge for me, as I had tried to stop many times before. Most times, I didn't even last one day! I never thought I would be able to stop; I thought I was going to be a smoker until the day I died. I had a super addictive personality and had been smoking since I was twelve—almost fifteen years. Imagine trying to break a habit you've had for fifteen years, let alone the addictive substance to contend with on top of it!

I *really* wanted to stop. Just like the other twenty-plus times I had tried and failed.

I wish I could tell you there was some magic formula I went through that helped me stop, but there wasn't. Everyone is different, and I can only tell you what helped me. When I stopped, I did it cold turkey. No gum, no patches, no nothing.

Except a change of mindset.

Your mindset is what will decide whether you stick to something or not. Whether it's stopping smoking, starting a business, or sticking to a diet, it all comes down to the way you talk to yourself.

When I stopped smoking, I said to myself, "I'm a nonsmoker." There was no "I'm trying to quit" or "I'm seeing how it goes." I shut the door. I was a nonsmoker. I didn't use verbiage like "quitting" or "giving up," as that would have implied that I was giving something up.

I wasn't giving anything up. I was purging something from my life for the better.

I literally told myself no when the thought of smoking entered my head.

The way you approach things is as important as the way you execute them. You've got to get your mind right and not doubt your resolve, not give yourself an out. So many people these days half-ass things and then wonder why they don't get the results they desire. I've been guilty of it myself in the past and still am sometimes. I catch myself talking myself out of things, justifying why I shouldn't work out, or explaining why I deserve that extra piece of cake!

It's human nature, but it's in these moments of weakness that we define ourselves.

When you stand fast during a moment of weakness, you are building up resilience, and it becomes easier to keep saying no. On the other side of the coin, when you give in to weakness, you are reinforcing that weakness, and it becomes harder to not give in again. That's why one slip can see you falling off the wagon entirely.

So there I was in 2017, with no experience and a burning will to make up for the time I had wasted. But that was all I needed. Motivation isn't enough to make you push through struggles. You need a *burning* desire to drive you forward, and that needs to come from within. Discipline will always trump motivation, and if you have a massive *why* driving you forward, discipline comes more easily. Motivation is great to start, but it won't see you to the finish line.

To help with this, I began to read a lot of books. Whenever I found a profound piece of advice or came to a realization myself, I would go onto Google Docs, type it up, print it out, laminate it, and put it on my wall.

I woke up to that wall every morning. The papers surrounded the monitor I worked on every day. That was my motivation—but like I said, motivation will only get you so far.

Once you are motivated, you need that desire to push you forward. When you desire something enough, you don't care if you feel like crap; you don't care how you feel. The desire simply kicks your butt and forces you forward no matter what.

Now at this point, my social skills were absolutely terrible; I could barely look anyone in the eye, let alone hold a conversation. I was so bad, I could not function in a normal job. I was on disability and could not work in a shop or factory, but I wasn't going to let that stop me. Nothing was going to stop me. So I started to learn the only option I thought I had: online marketing.

My mum had worked in digital marketing back in 2001, so I knew it was possible to make money online. So I dove into digital marketing, thinking I could become successful from behind my computer screen and never have to talk to anyone or show my face (didn't quite work out like that, as you will see)!

But making the switch to online marketing wasn't easy. My head was filled with thousands of hours of video game knowledge and not much else. But I was determined. I stopped playing video games and started learning everything I could. Every day, I woke up, turned on the computer, and went to work. I was more motivated than I had ever been in my life.

In January 2017, I read a book for the first time in over a decade. In February 2017, I made my Facebook profile, signed up for a $1,000 course on a maxed-out credit card, and learned everything I could about digital marketing. I studied every day; I was obsessed. I wanted to make up for all the time I had wasted. I bought a six-month subscription to a popular page builder that included another course on digital marketing. I watched all the videos and tried to replicate what I saw. While I was following that course, I bought a few other courses and continued to learn as much as I could.

I was learning and trying, learning and trying, but it felt like I was getting nowhere.

The most important thing was that I was actually taking action. So many people get stuck in learning mode when they should be in implementing mode. If you're forever stuck in analysis paralysis and never take any action, you'll never succeed.

For six months, I relentlessly pursued redemption. I spent countless hours just trying to get a foothold and gain some traction. It was exhausting.

I tried to build up my social media presence with quotes, and I was getting crickets.

I tried to run ads for clients as an agency but was too terrified to jump on a call to discuss their proposals and close deals.

I tried to open my own e-commerce store only to find there was way too high of a startup cost.

I tried so many different things before I found something that worked for me.

I opened a few more credit cards, bought another course, and felt like I was still no closer to making any money.

Then I discovered affiliate marketing.

If you're not familiar with what affiliate marketing is, let me give you a brief overview. With affiliate marketing, your main job is to find someone with a problem, and then to find someone else who develops and maintains a product that is a solution to the problem. That's it. You connect the person who needs the service with the person who provides the service, and you, the affiliate marketer, get paid.

In my opinion, affiliate marketing is the best and easiest business model when done the right way. But back then, I didn't know what the right way was. At first, I tried a few different products. I tried selling software, I tried selling on Amazon, I tried selling courses. I created some websites with helpful tips linking to various affiliate groups. I got kicked out of some Facebook groups for sharing my affiliate link in their groups, something I later learned was a big no-no. I tried paid ads and was just throwing money at the wall to see what stuck. I was making nothing.

The danger zone was looming, and I was running out of money *fast*.

I was way in the red, and after spending thousands trying to learn what worked, I was running out of options.

When you get to this level, you only have two options.

You can quit, and everything you have endured, spent on, and pushed through over the last however many days, weeks, months, or years can be for nothing. You can look for an escape, change your direction, and start again from square one.

Or you can continue to go all in and push that little bit more.

Everything in life is about mindset, and your resolve to carry on no matter the cost will give you the best chance at succeeding in whatever you put your mind to. I could have easily looked at my bank balance and the countless hours I had spent over those six months with little to show for it and said, "I'm done; this isn't working. Let's quit." I didn't. I said, "I am going to make this work, no matter what." Failure was not an option for me: in my mind, I had nothing to fall back on.

What was the alternative? Go through the arduous journey of something brand new and make the last six months be for nothing? Go back on benefits and piss my life away on video games forever?

I wasn't willing to accept that fate.

The problem for most people is that they can go back to comfort, or at least a more comfortable scenario than what they have now. Unless you are incredibly strong-willed, you will quit when times get tough if you have something to fall back on. When you have no other option, you don't give up when it gets hard or uncomfortable or someone tells you to start being realistic and get a "normal" job. You battle it through to the end and keep attacking it until you start to see the results you want. That is what winners do, and that grit is the only thing that separates the winners from the quitters.

In July 2017, things started clicking for me when I discovered a new way to do affiliate marketing.

Most people who try affiliate marketing go about it the wrong way: they try to promote Amazon products or physical products for a measly 2 or 3 percent commission. This can create great income for people who already have blogs, huge audiences, or influence, but it is really hard for the beginner to get started this way.

What's worse, people who take this route only promote one-time commission products. The problem with this is you continually have to be making sales every month for income to come in, and you spend most of your time promoting yourself for peanuts.

This is the *hardest* way to do affiliate marketing for beginners.

I learned there are three golden rules you want to stick by when choosing your main product of choice:

1. It needs to be a recurring product, meaning you get paid every month for the lifetime of the product.

2. It needs to have a high lifetime value. We want people to stick around and pay for years to come, right? That means the product has to be a great tool or service that people will keep paying for.

3. It needs to be an eternal product in a consistent niche—
    something that is still going to be around in five or
    ten years.

If you're interested in learning more about affiliate marketing and
how to find products that fit into these three golden rules, scan the
following QR code:

In August 2017, I found a great product I believed in that ticked all
three of these boxes. I made my first commission that month, and
another, and another. In that month, I made over $1,000.

It had been a long six months of trying and failing over and over again
to get to this point. Most people would have quit. Yet my desire to
make up for all the time I wasted outweighed the fear of failing. I
made $1,000 the next month too! In October, I made $2,000, and it
just grew from there! Less than a year after trying to take my own
life, I was one of that company's *top* affiliates.

Just think about that for a moment. What other industry allows you
to advance like that?

From nothing. No college, no experience.

How many people do you know who spend five or even ten years in a company and never get recognized or advanced?

It was at that moment I realized I had made my dream a reality.

I could finally support myself, I was worth so much more than I thought for so many years, and I was only just beginning to tap into my full potential.

Can you imagine where I would be now if I had quit on that fifth month and twenty-ninth day?

After six months of getting nowhere and making no progress, it can be very tempting to quit, and most people do. Most people will quit at the first sign of hardship and find any excuse to quit to slink back into comfort.

Perseverance is key. Even though I was earning good money, this time wasn't all smooth sailing either. While I was learning and building my business, my mum was in and out of the hospital, and in March 2017, she almost died due to a close call with sepsis. So on top of all the stresses and discomfort of changing myself, I was in and out of the hospital, facing the prospect of losing the person I cared about the most.

But I stuck with the work. I had made a promise to myself that I was going to change, and I meant to keep that promise.

CHAPTER 5

Finding Success in Those First Six Months

I want to pause my story here and share with you in more detail how I succeeded in these first six months. I think those months were crucial in helping me break the patterns of living I had formed over the years, and I hope they can help you too.

One of the most impactful habits I adopted was reading. I used to hate reading books, as I found them boring and laborious. Yet I knew one of the most important skills of any high achiever was reading. I searched online for the best business and entrepreneurial books I could find. One stood head and shoulders above the rest.

Think and Grow Rich has been dubbed by many as the "Entrepreneur's Bible," and it certainly had a huge impact on me the first time I read it. Inside, author Napoleon Hill details thirteen success principles he learned from dedicating his life to researching success and conducting more than 500 interviews with the most successful people on the planet. If you implement even one of Hill's success principles in your own life, you will see a dramatic change.

I believe much of my success came from at least five of Napoleon Hill's success principles from *Think and Grow Rich*:

First, I had a **burning desire.** I was sick of doing the same thing over and over, sick of playing games just to get false highs that were getting shorter and shorter lived. I had a burning desire to make up for all the years I wasted and make something of myself.

If you don't have a burning desire to make a change, then you won't. It can't just be a thought or a want. It needs to be an all-consuming desire you will keep gravitating toward.

Second, I made a **definite decision.** I didn't try hundreds of different things before I found my success. I decided what I wanted to do, and I stuck at it until I found success.

Stick with one thing and don't give up. Do not jump from affiliate marketing to e-commerce to Amazon to agency, and then jump from subniche to subniche inside them. The biggest killer of dreams is shiny object syndrome, and it can be so easy to fall into.

Shiny object syndrome is where you constantly jump onto the next fad—"shiny object"—that is being promoted. These days, it's harder than ever to keep our concentration on one objective because we are being bombarded with "the next and best thing," and many people fall for it. A week after finding a new shiny object, they're already bored and seeking the next thing, and the next, and the next.

Have you ever heard the saying, "If you chase two rabbits, you will catch none"? It is true: stick to one field and promote one program until you see solid success, and *then* think about diversifying. If I had gone all over the place and said, "I want to open a Shopify store," "I want to create my own product," "I want to do software development," "I want to create a course," or "I want to sell this," I would probably still be chasing multiple rabbits with no success.

Third, I **persisted**. It took me six to seven months before I found my place and started making progress. But forget six months, six weeks, six days, or even six hours. Some people quit as little as six minutes into trying something new!

I persisted for six months before I had success with affiliate marketing. I stuck with one program and was making over $5,000 a month before I started promoting other programs.

In other words, don't give up. I was motivated by my burning desire to change. What was my alternative? Go back into bad habits, start playing computer games, and spend my time in a make-believe world where nothing matters? *Screw that,* I told myself. *I am never going back to that; I am never doing that again. I am going to keep going and keep persisting until I make something of myself.*

There was no other option for me, I was not going to stop, and I refused to kick back until I made it and was satisfied. As I write these words, I now know that day isn't going to come, because I have got a heck of a lot of people to inspire, motivate, and teach to Taylor Their Best Life.

Fourth, I gained **specialized knowledge**. I learned everything there was to know about the platform I was working with, and I knew more than anyone. If I didn't know the answer to something, I would find the answer.

Finally, I had total and utter **faith**. Despite almost everyone around me thinking I couldn't do it, I held my faith and believed I could. When I started seeing success, everyone who had doubted me before started congratulating me.

There are many other books I read in my first year as an entrepreneur and many I would recommend to you. Scan this QR code for my full recommended reading list:

When I first got started, I was a shell of a person. I was broken, I couldn't hold a conversation, and I had crippling anxiety. I was so nervous that I didn't even dare put a profile picture up on Facebook.

I never wrote anything original because I thought people would mock me, and my confidence was at an all-time low.

My fear of rejection and judgment paralyzed me from taking any action.

It took me months before I pushed myself to put a profile picture up, but I did because I knew it would help people connect with me.

Today, I don't even give a new profile picture a second thought. I just do it.

I don't worry about "what if" anymore; I just take action. I get so much more done, and it opens up so many more doors for me. Before, I calculated and overanalyzed everything, and now I just let it flow and make the most of everything.

I remember when I first started trying the agency thing. I would over-prepare just to talk to someone. I wrote down every possible question, scripted all my answers, and made sure I knew word-for-word how I would talk. I prepared for hours, drank seven cups of coffee, and built myself up to make a call.

When I finally built up the courage to make the call, they often didn't even answer, and we never connected again.

All of that prep, a whole day wasted preparing for something that did not happen. It's so silly, getting so worked up and planning out every little detail. It's not the end of the world if something goes wrong.

Now I just power through, and if I make a mistake, I shrug it off and keep plowing forward.

How much time do you waste every day worrying and overthinking things? Mark Twain said it best: "I've had a lot of worries in my life, most of which never happened." Stop worrying so much and just move forward, and what will be will be. You will get so much more done, have so many more opportunities, and life will just be so much simpler.

I'm not saying you can't ever get scared—I was constantly scared. Every step of the way was terrifying. But if you don't do things that scare the crap out of you, you will never become your best self.

If you don't take the first step, you can't take the next step.

One of my first steps was simply putting a profile picture up on Facebook. I remember this photo very well because it took me an hour to prepare for it. I put on a suit and a shirt, did my hair, and shaved. I took so many different photos, but I always looked too scared or too drowsy, like there was something not quite right. I second-guessed myself at every turn, went over things multiple times, and worried about every stray hair and clothing wrinkle. It took me an hour to do something that should have taken me ten minutes.

I must have taken about a hundred pictures before I found one that was "perfect." When it came time to upload my profile picture to Facebook, I was shaking. Sweat was beading down my forehead and every fiber of my being wanted to back down and not do it. Yet my fear of not living up to my full potential outweighed my fear of stepping up and stepping out of my comfort zone as I uploaded it.

Wouldn't you know it? I didn't die!

My fear had been completely unfounded, and no one made fun of me or made a nasty comment. In fact, no one made any comment at all. No one cared, and what I made up to be a mountain in my head was nothing but a molehill.

I felt that exact same paralyzing fear the first time I made an original post that wasn't a quote. It took me hours to write this post. I read it, reread it, and examined it with a fine-tooth comb to make sure nothing could be misunderstood and that it made total sense. Again, I was literally shaking and felt like my heart was going to explode when I clicked "post" for the first time and didn't delete it.

Yet again, I didn't die!

I learned something that day.

I learned that no one cares.

I don't mean this in a bad way: people are too concerned about how *they* are coming across to worry about what *you're* doing. You will focus on your own mistakes far more and far longer than anyone else and be your own worst critic.

Try and be your own best cheerleader instead.

So many people carry the scars of their childhood with them their entire lives. It can be brutal getting bullied and put down for the years you are supposed to develop the most. When we get to adulthood, we walk on eggshells and fear the ridicule and judgment we endured as children.

Yet for most people, they are not the same as adults as they were as children. Fellow adults have to deal with the real world and are way too worried about themselves to focus on every little misstep others make!

This leftover childhood fear stops us from taking action and stepping up. However, fear and embarrassment are temporary, but regret lasts a lifetime. I have a lot of regrets, and my main regret is the time I wasted locked away from the world for so many years because of past experiences. This is the regret of missed opportunities. I'm sure you know how bad the regret of a missed opportunity is, the regret of not taking action.

I may mess up, I may stutter, I may look like a fool, but it doesn't matter. We all regret the things we didn't do much more than the things we did do.

Plus, that first time is *always* the hardest.

That first post I made, the first time I went on camera, the first time I went to a meeting, the first time onstage, the first time leaving the country—they were all gut-wrenchingly terrifying things to do! My mind went into overdrive: *What if people think it's stupid? What if people think I'm stupid? Do I sound self-obsessed? Why would anyone care about what I have to say?* But I had to push it to the back of my mind and realize no one cared.

Even if people do think any of that, they're not likely to care or even remember it a month from now. People are too wrapped up in their own lives and how they are coming across to others to bother. We all dwell on our mistakes long after everyone else has forgotten them. Most people forget everything you have done and everything you have said unless it has a direct correlation to their own lives. They're simply too focused on themselves.

After the first time, it gets easier.

Gradually it gets easier every time.

Now, I often write things and don't even reread them before posting! Back in 2017, I would reread things a hundred times to make sure there weren't any mistakes. *Yes*, I may make some mistakes now and then, but I get a thousand more things done than I used to. If I make only five mistakes out of a thousand, that's still far more productive than overanalyzing and complicating every single decision.

Don't get me wrong. I have made some *bad* mistakes since 2017 with bad consequences, but the trick is to not dwell on them.

I own them and move on.

Ask any successful person and they will tell you if they had dwelled on bad decisions and mistakes they made, they would have never amounted to anything.

Again, it comes with practice.

Whenever I made even a *small* mistake in 2017, it was the end of the world. The sky was falling, and my anxiety made it feel like I was legitimately having a heart attack. But the more mistakes I made, the more I realized it wasn't as bad as I made it out in my head, and the more I found no one even remembered the times I felt like I was going to die of embarrassment.

Things will be much bigger in your own head than in anyone else's. Don't be so hard on yourself.

This success was just the beginning of what was to come. It used to pain me to think of all the time I wasted, all the opportunities I missed. I thought, *I've wasted my potential. I have no hope, it's too late, I'll never achieve anything now.* Really silly to think that at twenty-five years old, but the mind can play tricks on us.

After dropping out of college multiple times, missing years of school, and barely getting by on my exams, I thought my future was bleak. I focused on the negatives, fixating on the time wasted instead of looking to the future and all the time I *did* have left.

Can you relate?

You may think you haven't received what you deserve. I have done this in the past. I thought I had it bad and that I wasted my life. I was bitter, sour, and hurt that I was sexually abused as a child. I didn't think it was fair that all the other kids had dads and I didn't. I felt like I was destined for failure when I dropped out of college, and by the time I was twenty-two, I thought I had wasted all my opportunities.

Yes, I had it harder than a lot of people growing up, but I still had things to be grateful for, even though I didn't see it at the time. I didn't have any serious mental health issues that stopped my cognitive function. I wasn't starved. I didn't grow up in a third-world county. I was still breathing!

We all tend to think we're harshly mistreated in some way at some point and like to throw pity parties for ourselves. But the reality is if we have the ability to feel bad for ourselves, we really shouldn't feel that bad. If you have full control over your mental faculties, there's already something to be massively grateful for right there.

Before my overdose in 2017, I always looked at the negative and would question why things weren't better for me. Why wasn't I rich, why didn't I win the lottery, why had all these things happened to me, why, why, why? But I never did anything about it.

Let me tell you, coming close to death gives you a whole new outlook on life and makes you thankful for what you have. Being grateful for what you have is a big part of success. Focus on the positives, and you will attract more positives. Focus on the negatives, and more negatives will come to you.

It's easy to fall into the trap of self-pity, and here is how I like to put things in perspective: Imagine something bad really does happen. Imagine your spouse, mother, father, dog, or whatever is most dearest to you in the world is not here anymore. Vividly think about how that would feel.

Then come back to reality.

If you did it right, you will feel nothing but gratitude for still having them around, and it will put things in perspective for you.

It's never too late to do what you could have done. There's always hope. Sure, you may have been in a better position to start five years ago—you may have felt more stable, had better income, and been five years younger. Whatever! It doesn't matter. You can keep dwelling on the past and be in the same position a year from now, or you can start where you are and use what you have in front of you.

Harland Sanders found himself broke at the age of sixty-five but went on to found one of the most successful fast-food franchises on the planet. That's right: Colonel Sanders started franchising Kentucky Fried Chicken at sixty-five years old. Samuel L. Jackson didn't see much success until his part in *Pulp Fiction* at age forty-six, which he played while recovering from drug addiction. There are countless other stories of people reaching success well into their later years.

It's never too late unless you allow it to be too late.

I had achieved my goal of being able to support myself. What was next? Did I rest on my laurels and become satisfied? No! It would have been so easy at this point to just sit back and relax with my newfound success. Although I was happy with what I had managed to achieve, I was definitely not content to slip back into old habits. I had to keep going.

PART 3

STEPPING OUT AND STEPPING UP

CHAPTER 6

Stepping Out

At this point in my journey, my confidence was starting to grow, I was realizing that I had value to give, and I knew I was able to make money online.

However, many things weren't getting any easier.

The first time you do anything is always the scariest and hardest, and I was about to experience a lot of first times!

Because of my background, I was still scared every time I made a post or answered a question. Even today, I am generally quiet around people I don't know because that fear of what happened when I was a child is so embedded in my mind. Even after meeting thousands of awesome, friendly people and genuinely knowing and realizing there are more nice people in the world than there are mean, I still have that PTSD holding me back to a degree. My anxiety and social phobia are still very much present.

I've become very good at hiding my anxiety and fitting in. Moving to so many different homes as a child, I developed that chameleonlike defense mechanism where I could assimilate and act normal even though my anxiety was eating away at me.

Luckily, the Builderall community was a kind and welcoming community that never mocked me or put me down, even when I was wrong, which helped me conquer my fears.

Builderall is the program I have had the most success with since the start. They are an all-in-one marketing tool that builds websites, sends emails, hosts webinars, and more.

I started to build up quite a reputation in the community by answering questions in the groups and being the first to help whenever anyone needed anything. I studied the platform and lived in the training videos, and if anyone had a question, I would zoom off to find the answer in the training material or by trial and error.

Still never showing my face at this point, I wondered how I could make a name for myself even more.

That was when I decided to write the Builderall handbook, which would turn into a three-hundred-page document detailing all the features of Builderall and how to use its tools.

It took me more than one month of solid writing for over fourteen hours a day. I was obsessed. I was so excited about how many people it was going to help and how everyone would react to my incredible work. All I did was write, eat, and sleep.

Instead of selling the handbook to everyone, I gave it away for free. I didn't fully understand marketing at this point and just gave it away to help people. I could have used it to help build my client list or made it a limited-time offer. I simply gave it away to help and expected nothing in return.

I started getting great feedback in the group, and everyone was starting to see me as the go-to Builderall expert. That got me the attention of a lot of people, and at the end of October 2017, I was asked to speak at a summit—*live*.

By this point, I had done a handful of screen-share videos, and I literally had to pause after every sentence, sometimes midsentence, to keep myself together! When I was offered a chance to speak live for thirty minutes at a summit, my first reaction was, *There's no way I can possibly do this, nope, sorry, can't do it.* So I said no. I remember thinking to myself after the call ended, *What did you just do? This is your chance to make a name for yourself; this is your chance to shine.* "Lose Yourself" by Eminem started playing in the back of my mind.

Then I remembered a quote from Richard Branson that said, "If someone offers you an amazing opportunity and you're not sure you can do it, say yes and learn how to do it later."

So I called them back, said I would do it, and did just that.

I didn't have too long to learn because someone had dropped out due to illness and my speaking spot was now in less than two days. So I worked like crazy to prepare. I went to the store and bought a new microphone, a new camera, and a case of beer. I scripted the entire thing, practiced it, and had it down to a T. I was far too nervous to get out more than a sentence at a time freestyle!

So the day came and I was prepared. I drank about fifteen bottles of beer as a confidence boost. I had my printed-out script sitting just below the camera so it looked like I was looking into the camera when I was actually reading from the paper.

I got my presentation up, shared my screen, and started talking.

Something was wrong...

Everyone said they could barely hear me. I was talking and everyone was making ear gestures, and the host couldn't hear me either.

Panic set in, and my anxiety went into overdrive.

I was very good at appearing calm and collected on the outside while blowing a gasket on the inside and managed to keep my composure. We awkwardly went through some troubleshooting steps for about five minutes before the host told me to just continue. So I did my entire thirty-minute presentation with everyone's volume up to the max so they could hear me faintly. People were leaning in and trying hard to hear what I was sharing for the entire thirty minutes.

After the presentation was over and the pressure was off, I looked down and saw a red light on my microphone wire, and I quickly turned the same color.

I had done the entire presentation on mute and not realized!

To this day, I do not understand why they could faintly hear me. If they couldn't hear me at all, maybe I would have figured it out!

Yet instead of being laughed at and mocked, everyone was understanding. The host allowed me to come back over the weekend and do a rerecord for everyone. It was at this point I started to realize there were more nice people in the world than nasty—I had just been used to the nasty people most of my life.

Now imagine what would have happened to me if I had been in a less supportive community that knocked me down instead of building me up. If they hadn't allowed me to rerecord a week later, that great experience would have been a humiliating one. I sure wouldn't be anywhere near as far along as I am now!

That was another boost to my confidence, and I started posting even more online. I was answering questions and helping out more than ever before and became one of the most respected people in the community.

This was a stepping stone for what was yet to come.

If I had said no to this wonderful opportunity and growth experience, I probably would have also said no to speaking onstage, to traveling, and to going to events. Who knows where I would be now if I had said no to what at the time seemed like such a small event in my life.

My next challenge was also my next greatest achievement: the Certified Partners Program. Unlike the summit, this was an extended time on live calls with dozens of people for up to eight hours at a time. I was super nervous and had my camera off most of the time, or I would sit in the dark with my camera barely showing my face.

But during the Partners training, I made some of the best friendships I had ever made in my life. I was slowly opening back up and allowing people in after being shut off for so long. This is where I became great friends with many people, and two in particular whom I now consider to be family.

Erick Salgado is one of the best male role models I have ever had in my life. He has not only taught me a lot about digital marketing, but also how to be a decent human. "You always need to do the right thing, even when no one is looking," he told me on one of our chats in 2018.

Shelly Turner is one of my best friends, and I do not know anyone more giving than her. She has helped me through a few tough times over the years and always lends a hand to help out.

After a month of intense training and more pushing out of my comfort zone, I became the world's first Certified Partner for Builderall.

Unfortunately, my quick success was catching the attention of people I didn't want. I got into a toxic, narcissistic business partnership that almost consumed me. Like any narcissistic relationship, it started out great and quickly went downhill. I was out of the spotlight and fading into the background, and my partner received all the recognition.

It was clear to some people the kind of person he was. He was sneaky, underhanded, and willing to say or do anything to get his way, and I was a naive fool who fell for his consistent lies. He would always have an answer for everything. He would talk for hours about literally nothing and could have been the world's best politician.

During the next few months, he alienated half of the Certified Partners because of his actions, and it kicked my anxiety back into overdrive. Even though I was adored by many people, I felt like I was becoming more and more isolated again. My mind was playing tricks on me and telling me everyone hated me. It was getting to the point where I would stop posting on Facebook and stop talking in the meetings.

It was all in my head, of course. Sure, there were a couple of people who weren't impressed with me and resented me a bit, but that will happen wherever you go—you can't please and be loved by everyone. But the fear and paranoia in my head were forcing me to believe everyone suddenly hated and had forsaken me.

On Black Friday 2017, I purchased an incredible offer from my now great friends Omar and Melinda Martin. The offer was for their flagship training program, which was a great deal in itself, but it also included a ticket to a digital marketing event they were holding in Orlando, Florida, in April 2018.

I hadn't been on a plane in over fifteen years by this point, and the thought of going to an airport on my own scared the living crap out of me. Luckily, a friend I had met online agreed to meet me at the airport and show me around so I wouldn't be alone. Plus, my trusty old vice, beer, was always on tap for when I needed to calm down or get a confidence boost.

They say travel broadens the mind, and I wholeheartedly agree. America was such an exciting place to me. As my friend drove me around, I gazed out of the window, awestruck by the size of everything, how different it was from home, and the possibilities that lay ahead. I don't know if it was the sunshine, the humidity, or the energy from the people, but I felt more relaxed than I did back in the UK. Even today, I find people to be much more friendly and open in the US than in the UK.

A few days after I arrived in Orlando was the Commission Expo event I had flown over for. This was no Zoom meeting with a few dozen faces. This was real life, in person with a hundred people. I was so nervous, but I forced myself to show up every day.

I do, however, believe being nervous is good for two reasons. One, it means you're human. If you live your life without ever being nervous, then I'm pretty sure you're a sociopath! Two, it allows you to grow. If you are always in your comfort zone, then you never push yourself. You never know what you are capable of, and that's a tragic waste.

It's important to do something that scares you and pushes you to grow every single day. Otherwise, you'll never grow as a person.

At this point, I was pushing myself to the max.

After the breaks every day, they would hold a raffle, and on day two, I won one of the prizes. It was just after lunch, and even though most of the room was still empty at this point, my body felt rigid as a board as I walked up to receive it. My eyes widened, I awkwardly smiled, I grabbed my prize, and I slowly walked off the stage, my mind racing a million miles a minute and my blood pressure dropping. I barely made it back to my seat and thought I was going to pass out.

After a few weeks in Florida, I traveled up to Canada to work in person with my business partner. Looking back, there were some red flags, but I was too deep in to see them at the time. During my stay in Canada, I had some great times exploring with my business partner and his family. But most of the time was spent working like crazy. We rarely worked on anything I had thought of, and he always had some new idea that never turned into anything successful.

By this time, I was the seventh top affiliate in the world for Builderall. I remember thinking when I first started, *How am I ever going to get to the top?* There were many big names with thousands of sales, and I thought I would never be able to catch them. But with determination and faith, I managed to be seventh in the world just nine months after starting out. Today, I am the number one affiliate in the world for Builderall and a top affiliate for many other programs, earning millions of dollars as an online affiliate.

One of the biggest things that contributed to my success was failing at things—messing up and just getting back up and trying something else. If you're consistently worrying about consequences and falling down, you will never go for it and get anything done. I got to the point where I could constantly attack things, which meant I got ten times more done than someone who wondered and worried about the consequences. It was a hard lesson to learn after being so harshly punished for my mistakes growing up.

I had spent almost five months with my business partner in Canada when Erick reached out to me. Because I was one of the most respected people in the Builderall community and a rapidly advancing top affiliate, Erick invited me to speak onstage in Italy at the very first Builderall Everest event. It was a digital marketing event Erick had created, and the premise was simple: "Everest, the highest point in digital marketing." There was no selling; this would be a pure value event. Contrary to 99 percent of other events out there, Erick cared more about serving people than making money.

The thought of speaking on a stage terrified me.

I had never spoken in front of more than a few people before, and even the thought of being in a room having a normal conversation with five or more people scared the crap out of me. This was an extended talk in front of one hundred people, and the focus was all going to be on me.

When I read his invitation, I froze. My eyes widened and my entire body went tingly. I was like a deer in the headlights.

After a few moments, I snapped out of it and said yes. I knew it was an awesome opportunity, and I didn't want to look like a coward in front of Erick. Erick was and still is one of the best male role models in my life, and I have the utmost respect and admiration for him.

After learning I was offered a spot to speak in Italy, my partner said he wanted me to stay in Canada to work on "our" projects and my speaking engagement wasn't as important. He begged me to stay, claiming we were so close to completing projects, I couldn't do anything else until we finished work on them.

This is what narcissists do: they try to keep you isolated as much as possible so you become dependent on them.

I was getting sick of working on my partner's ideas all the time and slaving away with nothing to show for it. I had done more by myself in the last three months of 2017 than I had in the entirety of 2018 working with him.

Luckily for me, my past experiences made me strong enough to resist, and I was adamant I was going to Italy to speak. Thank God I had the strength to say, "No, I am going to do what I want to do."

He had tried to grind me down and had not succeeded. He had always said our decisions needed to be group decisions to try and take away my power and then make those decisions himself. There was always some crazy reason as to why it was one rule for him and one for me, but he was so good at making it sound true.

I booked my flights and was all ready to have a brief stint back in the UK before flying directly to Italy. Yet a short time before my flight, something told me to check on the status of my flight. Call it a sixth sense, a higher power, or what have you, but something drew me to check at that moment.

I went to the airline's website, and it was gone!

I searched online and it turned out the airline I had booked with had gone into administration! No email, no message, no notification, just gone! With less than two weeks until the event in Italy, I went into a frenzy trying to source another affordable flight. I had to book something *fast*.

I was making okay money at this point but still flying by the seat of my pants most months. I wasn't putting anything away and still had a mountain of credit card debt because I was spending everything I earned on business, traveling, and ads.

By the grace of God, Air Canada was offering a discount for anyone who had been affected by the other airline's collapse, and I scraped just enough together to make it there. If something hadn't told me to log in to check my flight time, I would have never known, the low rates would have been gone, and I would never have rebooked in time.

Call it fate, call it destiny, call it sheer luck!

Whatever you want to call it, something had a hand in guiding me that day. I was obviously on the right path.

If it wasn't for that fateful moment, I may never have shared my story, never saved some lives from suicide, and never impacted tens of thousands of people around the world.

Sometimes, you have got to think there's Someone or Something looking over you to guide you where you're meant to go.

CHAPTER 7

The Turning Point: Fear Your Regrets

It's strange to be at an event where you are one of the stars. People are watching you and walking up to introduce themselves. I had been to a couple of events by this point, but I was used to fading into the background and going unseen. This was a whole different vibe. I also usually sat at the back of the room. I didn't like people sitting behind me and always made a point of sitting as close to the back as possible. This time, I had an assigned seat at the very front.

I remember staring at the stage, afraid to turn around and make eye contact with anyone. I wasn't sure what I wanted to speak about. I could have spoken about Facebook, Google Ads, traffic, funnels, or a plethora of topics I had become proficient in. However, I was experiencing major imposter syndrome, and I felt like I didn't have any value to give. So I decided to talk about my journey, my story, and where I had come from. Keeping it very surface level, I spoke about battling anxiety, depression, and the social phobia I suffered with. I had no intentions of sharing my suicide attempts or anything deeper.

I was so nervous the night before, I practiced my whole speech five or six times. I stood in front of the mirror and rehearsed over and over until three in the morning. Just like the summit, I scripted every word and practiced until I knew it word for word. I had a notepad of my speaking cues, with a word or two for each topic to remind me.

The big day was upon me, and I was absolutely terrified. I contemplated just running away, or saying I was too sick to talk. Yet the fear of letting down Erick, Shelly, and everyone there outweighed the fear of everything else. If I ran, I would look like a coward. If I refused, I would look like a dick. If I called in sick, I would let myself and everyone around me down, and that wasn't going to happen.

I had felt the bitter sting of regret most of my life. I never took action due to fear and had run away when I should have stayed and fought. That ate at me for years: the coward I had become and the resentment I had held toward myself for being a coward all that time.

Failure was not an option.

At lunch, I drank a bottle and a half of wine to help calm my nerves and give me that confidence boost I needed. I was the second speaker after lunch, and despite the alcohol, I was still terrified.

I kept trying to convince myself everything was going to be fine. I had practiced, I knew exactly what to say, and it was only a short talk. Yet when the nerves kicked in, all that preparation and practice went out the window. I had to bring my notebook onstage with me.

I felt like I didn't do a great job, yet everyone was hanging on my every word. There were gasps from the audience. Some people were crying and everyone looked shocked. There was applause every minute, and I felt a sense of acceptance that was new to me.

I still remember the looks on Erick and Shelly's faces as I told my story for the first time.

Erick's face was deep in concentration; I could tell he was really feeling the story and taking it all in. He looked genuinely concerned, impressed, and almost flabbergasted by the story I was telling.

Shelly's face was the opposite: she was beaming, proud of my accomplishments and the circumstances I had risen from.

Both Erick and Shelly have always been proud to see me grow from where I was to where I am today.

As I got to the end of my speech, the crowd all stood up and cheered for me.

It wasn't because I performed well or had charisma or any of that stuff. It was the fact they could see me breaking through before their eyes. The fact I had not stood up and spoken in front of three people before, let alone a hundred. The fact I was being vulnerable and sharing my personal struggles and hurdles that most people were too afraid to share.

I put the recording online so you can view the entire thing on my YouTube channel here:

It wasn't the best performance, but many have told me it was inspiring to see me up there despite my fears.

As I walked back to my seat, I was shaking, my heart felt like it was going to burst through my chest, and I could feel tears welling up.

Yet I held it in. All the years of abuse, struggle, and turmoil meant I could hold more in than anyone ever should.

I should have broken down there and cried. If I had conquered my fear completely and didn't care what anyone else thought, I would have. It was the fear of being emotional in front of others that stopped me. But crying and being vulnerable would have helped my growth even more because I was in a safe, supportive environment.

My strong mind holds me back because where I should reach my limit, break down, and allow room for growth, I just don't. I hold it in, and hold it in, and hold it in some more.

If you want to grow as a person, you need to be broken down in order to be built back up—but in the right environment. Just as a muscle gets broken and torn to grow back stronger, so does our mind.

Yet this was a great victory.

I had broken through many fears and my barriers. I hadn't folded. I hadn't failed, and I felt like I could do anything. No longer was my past defined by being a cowardly lowlife, afraid to act and afraid to speak up. No, this was my new defining moment and the first time in a long time I felt like I had courage.

Stepping out into the unknown, allowing yourself to be vulnerable, and pushing out of your comfort zone is one of the hardest things to do, but it's also the most rewarding. Outside your comfort zone is the growth zone. If you never venture out of your comfort bubble, then you never grow as a person. You stay the same, never reaching your full potential, and that's a tragic waste.

Most people are not willing to allow themselves to be vulnerable, to let people see their human sides. We live in a time where people share all the best bits of their lives and hide the rest, so we think we must do the same. But it's the people who are truly comfortable showing the good and the bad who are going to succeed.

Everything you want is on the other side of fear. Feel the fear, and do it anyway.

A lot of people see me doing my thing onstage and at weekly meetings and think, *Whoa he's confident. I wish I could be like him.* The opposite is true. I am not confident—far from it. I'm leaps and bounds ahead of where I was when I began, but I'm still far away from where I want to be.

Every time I think about speaking, a thousand doubts come into my head: *What if I stutter, what if I make a fool of myself, what right do I have to talk about this, what if no one cares, what if, what if, what if?* Even after speaking onstage in nine different countries and being on countless Zoom calls, I still feel the fear.

Yet I don't let it stop me.

That speech in Italy was far from my best performance. I stood on the stage without much movement and practically read from the notebook in my hand. Yet I'd never done it before, and I openly said at the beginning that I was super nervous about telling part of my story.

You aren't expected to do a stellar job the first time you do something. You don't get in a car the first time and expect to race Formula One. When you're born, you can't walk. You don't try walking a couple of times and go, *I failed a few times. This walking thing isn't for me!* You keep trying: you start to crawl, and then you start to walk, and you fall down hundreds of times along the way before you perfect the technique.

It's the same thing for anything. Expect to fall down and get scrapes and bumps, but approach it as a toddler approaches walking. Pick yourself back up, and take those few more steps, getting better each time you try.

As we get older, we become more self-conscious about our failures and let other people tell us what our limits are. Sometimes, family members tell us we need to be realistic and not aim so high. They mean well because they don't want to see us let down or hurt, but they hold us back. We need to push all that to the side and have the courage to say, "*No*. I am capable of anything I damn well please. I respect you trying to protect me, but stop. I am going for this thing, and I am not going to stop until I get it, no matter how many times I fall down."

Only with the attitude of a baby learning to walk will you become good at something you are bad at.

That night, I couldn't sleep, and I began to think of all the opportunities I had missed due to fear. I felt the regrets, the pain, and the anguish of letting opportunities and relationships I loved slip through my fingers because I was too afraid to pursue them. I imagined being ninety years old on my deathbed, cold and alone, bitter and resentful from the life I had created. This feeling was the worst pain I had ever felt. I vowed there and then that no matter how scared I was, I was *never* going to say no because of fear ever again.

Sadly, anxiety and depression don't work that way, and my transformation was not an instantaneous one. Still I was making great progress. I used to be so scared to do anything. I hesitated, overthought, and was so worried about what other people thought of me that it took me ten times longer to do something than everyone else, and often, I would miss out on what I was aiming for.

But now, I had a much bigger fear, a fear I want to instill in you.

Many people have a plethora of fears, especially when it comes to new business opportunities. Fear of the unknown. Fear of failing. Fear of looking stupid. Fear of things "not working out."

We already know fear is a much bigger motivating factor than reward.

What is your biggest fear in the world right now? For many people, it's death. Surprisingly, for even more people, it's public speaking!

My biggest fear is how I'm going to feel on my deathbed.

You see, fear and embarrassment are temporary. Regret lasts a lifetime! Think back to a time you were fearful or embarrassed. I bet most of those things from the past won't register much on your radar. Now, think back to a regret you have. I'm betting there are a few that still sting.

Fear and embarrassment, although they can feel horrific at the time, don't last anywhere near as long as regret. Many times, the fear of something like public speaking is all in our heads, and when we feel embarrassed, other people don't even notice or care.

The feeling of regret, however, is very real! Missing out on something, not seizing the moment, having someone or something you want pass you by because you were too afraid to take action? That hurts! Knowing and living with the fact that things could have been different is very tough. That's why you need to take action in spite of fear.

All the wonderful opportunities I have grasped over the last few years could have so easily been passed up due to fear. The first video, the first live meeting, the first online summit, and the first time speaking onstage? I almost said no to them all because of fear!

Yes, there has been a lot of fear, and there have been some embarrassing moments—*very* embarrassing moments. But if I hadn't said yes, where would I be right now? Nowhere near as far along, I can assure you!

I want to instill a new fear in you. A fear that has kept me from running off the stage. A fear that has forced me to show up and do my best when all I wanted to do was hide. A fear that can push you to do things that you never thought possible.

Picture this...

Imagine being at the end of your life and knowing you were capable of so much more. Look back on your life at all the missed opportunities and all the chances you didn't take. How would you feel if you knew you could have made a difference in the world? That what you cared about most could have been saved or taken care of better? Yet instead of rising up and becoming your best self, you flushed it down the drain and let down everything you cared about most.

I can't think of any more horrific way to feel than that.

Want to know what I fear? I fear being in the same place next year as I am right now. I fear *not* trying and never taking the shot. I fear being old and regretting all the things I could have done and not doing them. I fear missing out on who I am meant to become. I fear not living up to my potential. I fear not living my best life. I fear not having a positive impact on the world. I fear ending up on my deathbed regretting all the shots I didn't take. These are my fears, and they push me to push myself every day.

I already wasted ten years of my life; I'm not wasting any more. Talk to anyone near the end of their life, and they will tell you they regret the things they didn't do far more than the things they did.

Some of you may be quite happy and content where you are, and if so, good on you! But if there's even an ounce of you that knows deep down you were meant for more in this world, stop letting the wrong kind of fear stop you from reaching your potential, and start taking action!

Once you put things into perspective like this, then that time you forgot what you were saying on a live call, that time you tripped on the stage, any time you messed up, however big or small—none of it matters. Because as long as we are showing up and doing our best each and every day, who gives a damn about the mistakes we make along the way?

Want to know the "big secret" that helped me succeed so fast?

The big secret is...

There are no secrets.

You have everything you need to break through and get to the next level in your business and life right now. Everything! There's only one thing that's stopping you. *Fear* is what is holding you back right now, but it's the wrong kind of fear. You need to use fear to your advantage instead of letting it control you.

I still feel fear every time I step on a stage and do a live call. I feel the fear and do it anyway because of my much bigger fears.

I felt fantastic for a few days after my speech in Italy, but my anxiety was not gone. Far from it. I still struggled with eye contact, was nervous during conversations, and clammed up completely around new people. I felt like a pretender. A fake.

I had just done one of the most incredible things of my life. I spoke in front of a hundred people about fear and overcoming it, but I still felt anxious around new people.

Why did I still feel this way? When was my anxiety going to subside? What was it going to take? Would I ever be able to have a carefree conversation with a stranger? Would I ever be normal? Would I ever be free of it?

Two weeks after my first speech in Italy, I flew to Germany to speak again. I told the same story and got another standing ovation and great feedback.

But something else amazing happened as well.

There was a lady there who spoke right after me. It was her first time onstage, and she was really nervous. She was touched by my story and found it inspiring. After her speech, she told me she had felt like running offstage, and it was my story and courage that helped her to stay.

At the time, I was very happy about it and proud my story had helped someone.

Yet I didn't yet see the larger picture.

Her speech had helped and inspired others to go on and do great things, too. She then went on to speak more, and who knows how many other people's lives she touched?

Since then, I've employed the philosophy of reaching just one person. It doesn't matter if 99 percent of the room doesn't like me. If I can just reach that one person and inspire them to greatness, then who knows how many millions of lives will be affected for the better because of that one person and the ripple effect they'll create?

CHAPTER 8

Regaining Control

I went back to the UK for a short time and was not greeted with happiness. In 2017, my mum had stepped on a tack and sliced her foot open. Not a big deal for most people, but since she was diabetic and had bad circulation, it never healed, and she ended up wheelchair bound.

While I was away, Mum was in and out of the hospital with sepsis, and no one told me how bad it had gotten. She was not getting the care she needed, and the house was in a terrible state. On top of that, she had taken in one of her friend's children because they were in a bad way.

When I came back, my room and every other room in the house looked like it had been trashed. It was like one of those houses you see on *Hoarders*. Not only that, but my chair and bed were damaged and burnt beyond repair, and money and collectibles had been stolen. It stank with a heavy odor of animals, rot, and mold.

My mum had been in a downward spiral for years, slipping deeper into depression after losing her house back in 2009 in an unfair lawsuit. By this time she had pretty much given up, and if it weren't for her children, she wouldn't have been alive anymore.

My brothers weren't great at tidying up or taking care of anything because my mum had never instilled discipline in them over the years. In fact, I was the only one who told them to do anything, which made them hate me even more.

Like I said at the beginning, we can't blame others for the way they were raised. My brothers were raised the way they were because of the way Mum was raised, and because of the way my grandparents were raised, and so on. It's a vicious circle until we find the courage and drive to break it. Until you become aware of your surroundings and influences instead of blindly being controlled by them, it's impossible to change.

As I write these words, we have all broken the cycle and are doing great by anyone's standards, but back then, we were still a recovering dysfunctional family.

My mum didn't know I was coming back until the day before. When I arrived, she was trying to tidy up so I wouldn't feel so bad. That made my blood boil: there were three capable teenagers in the house, and my wheelchair-bound mum was tidying up so it didn't look so bad when I got back.

Instead of getting angry, I simply told her to stop and started tidying up myself.

Once upon a time, I would have exploded into orbit, wrecked things even more, screamed at my brothers, and destroyed my relationships in a fit of rage—but I was no longer a bitter, sad, isolated failure. I felt a sense of control and capability I hadn't ever felt.

In a way, I'm thankful I went into foster care and children's homes, because if I hadn't, I wouldn't have learned to be as capable as I am today. I wouldn't wish my struggles on anyone, but having discipline and enduring these hardships growing up have made me more capable than everyone around me when I put my mind to it. For years, I was too numb to attempt anything, yet when I started to try, I realized I was more capable than I had dreamed.

Less than a month later, I was traveling again, this time to Brazil to speak in front of four hundred people! I was feeling more relaxed around other people the more I went out; speaking at all these events was instrumental in me becoming who I am today. The fear of failing and feeling the sting of regret again pushed me forward and kept me saying yes to these opportunities.

I am so grateful for all the opportunities I have been given over the last few years, and even more grateful for all the times I said yes. There were so many times I could have said no and so many times I almost did. If you remember, I actually did say no to speaking at the online summit originally and then found the courage to call back and say yes.

If I hadn't had the courage to say yes to making that first post on Facebook...

I would never have had the courage to say yes to speaking at the summit...

I would then never have had the courage to get on a plane for the first time in fifteen years...

I would then have never had the courage to speak onstage in front of four hundred people in Brazil and go on to do all the wonderful things I've done in the last few years.

Like I've said before, the first time is always the hardest, and it's amazing how one small action can snowball and push you to make the next step and the next. Never underestimate the power of a small, seemingly insignificant action. The courage you grow from that action could be integral to your next steps.

I am a firm believer in doing something each day that scares you, so seek out opportunities that make you nervous. They will help you realize what is possible. Things I am doing now were not even on my radar a few years ago. I *never* thought I would ever do any public speaking. Heck, three years ago, I couldn't even put a profile picture up on Facebook!

If you always feel comfortable and safe, then you will never reach your full potential and find out what you are capable of. And that is a tragic waste. There are so many little things like this that have catapulted me on to success, things that seemed small or insignificant yet had a *massive* impact on where I am today. Never say no to an opportunity, no matter how much of an inconvenience or struggle it might be.

It was a huge inconvenience for me to spend my own money to go to all of these places and speak. I put every penny I had back into my business and lived way below my means for years because I was grasping every opportunity I could, no matter the cost. But thank God I had the courage to say yes, because if I didn't, I could have easily turned down any and all of these amazing opportunities due to doubt, limiting beliefs, and fear. That may have seemed like the easy route at first, but it would have left me in the same position I was in before—and that would not have been so easy.

If you make the easy choices, your life will be hard, but if you make the hard choices, your life will be much easier in the end.

It's incredible what we are capable of when we remove the belief patterns we have come to accept as reality. Once you remove those barriers, you will be shocked at what you can accomplish. Whatever your reality, you have the power inside yourself to achieve what you want to achieve.

If I can come from where I was in 2017 to where I am now, then just imagine what you can do!

It was an incredible few months of traveling to all of these different places. Five days after Brazil, I was back in the US speaking in Memphis. These few months were where I experienced most of my growth. In less than a year, I went from being afraid of putting up a profile picture on Facebook to speaking in front of four hundred people—without a notepad this time! It's incredible what we can do when we push our comfort zones to the max and take action in spite of fear.

Every event I spoke at, there were a number of people in tears. Some people would come up to me at the end of my speech and thank me for speaking up and sharing. I didn't realize the severity of it yet, or the significance, but my opening up was helping others through their own struggles and trauma. It wasn't until a little bit later I realized the true impact my speeches were having on some people.

I was feeling more and more in control of my life and my emotions and felt safer around others. However, that control was about to be pushed to its limits yet again.

I spent Christmas with the family and prepared for another trip to the US in January 2019, this time to Los Angeles for a cruise. This was a Marketers Cruise I had booked with my business partner all the way back in April 2018, when I was working in Canada with him.

My old partner and I shared a small cabin together on the cruise: this was where he slipped up and I saw plain as day the type of person he was. He was drunk on the cruise, and he thought he could confuse and manipulate me. He didn't count on me being so coherent and functional after so much alcohol, and I caught his manipulation red-handed. I am not shy when I have had a lot of drinks, and I confronted him and told him I saw him for exactly who he was.

He stormed off, and then the next day, it was like nothing had ever happened.

That was the day I stopped working on his constant stream of rubbish ideas and started silently moving everything into my own brand. But I couldn't leave our business together outright: he had me locked in. He had had me sign documents and other legal stuff, which left me trapped.

I knew I needed to find a way out, and I simply told him, "I am sick of working on stuff that nothing ever comes from." He knew I wasn't happy, but he still used the contract between us and our shared assets to stay together.

I would have to tolerate his presence for a few more months yet.

During the cruise, I had some good news. I got a phone call saying they had found my father.

A year or so earlier, my mum had a heart-to-heart talk with me about my father. For years, she'd told me many different stories about him: he left six months after I was born, he left a few weeks after I was born, and so on. I always thought my father knew about me, that he could reach out to me at any time and that he chose not to. But during this talk, my mum told me he left months *before* I was born and may not have even known about me.

So I set out to find him. How could I blame him if he didn't even know I existed?

I did some research but turned up nothing until I hired some professionals to do the job. While I was on the cruise, I got a phone call: "We've found him!" I had no idea if he was even alive before this.

Great! Let's get to work, I thought. I was happy, scared, anxious, and nauseated all at once.

When I got back from Los Angeles, I went straight to an event in

Brighton. From there, I drove five hours across the bottom of the country to find him.

I wrote a letter to hand to him, as I could not bring myself to speak the words without breaking down or losing my temper. If he rejected me on the spot or reacted in a way I didn't like, there was no telling how I would respond in the heat of the moment, and I wasn't going to waste everything I had worked so hard for by potentially landing myself in prison.

I decided to personally hand him the letter for a couple of reasons:

1. I could ask who he was so I could make sure the letter was being placed in his hands, and I would know if he had been ignoring me. If I sent the letter, I would be wondering if it even got to him.

2. I knew he had a family, and I didn't want the letter to be opened or read by another member of the family and cause any problems for them.

I found him, spoke to him, handed him the letter, and waited around for a few hours to see if he would call.

He didn't.

I drove back up with the understanding that I had just given him huge news. He would have to adjust, but I had high hopes that he would come around. A month went by: nothing. I started to have doubts, and my mind raced with thoughts of inadequacy. I pushed them to the back of my mind and carried on.

About two months later, I still hadn't heard anything. That was more than long enough for a response, so I decided to send another letter. It didn't take long for him to respond this time! Two days after he signed for the letter, I got a phone call.

He was very abrupt and to the point. He told me there was no way he could be my father and to stop sending him letters because he couldn't have them coming to the house.

My initial response? Anger, sadness, resentment, revenge: the typical, bitter reactions to rejection. I thought, *I'll send letters to you and your whole family until I find the truth*. The "I'm gonna hurt you ten times more" response.

Then something came over me. I had an epiphany: it was pointless. My feelings of anger diminished and I realized…

He wasn't around the years I needed him the most, and I sure didn't need him anymore! Why let the actions of someone I had only just met control my thoughts? He was missing out a hundred times more than I was by not knowing me. He proved that by his character.

Again, I felt in control and able to rationally react to the situation without popping a blood vessel.

This was a really big step for me, as a couple of years ago, my reaction would have been a *lot* different. Now, I feel fine. It is what it is, as they say, and there's no point dwelling on it. Maybe it's for the better.

We all experience rejection at some point. Some of us experience more than others. Rejection can cripple you or motivate you. Rejection crippled me to the point where I wouldn't even try for the longest time. Growing up is the time where rejection hits you the hardest. Your adolescent mind starts questioning everything: *Am I good enough? What's wrong with me? I don't have anything of value to say or give.*

Rejection is going to happen whether you like it or not, and it doesn't change when you grow up, either.

What can change is how you react to it.

When you next experience rejection, before you go all Bruce Banner or start to question yourself, take a moment and reflect on whether it's worth it to respond negatively. The only person's opinion about you that matters is *yours!* Don't let other people live in your head rent-free, just be your *awesome* self! Not everything is meant to be, no matter how much we will it to be.

Upon returning to the UK, Erick asked Michael, another member of Builderall, and me to host an Everest event in the UK. I thought this would be a great opportunity to grow the Builderall user base in the UK, and it would be cool to host my own event.

March was insane, and I was working around the clock to bring everything together for the event. I had seriously underestimated how much time, energy, effort, and logistics went into live events.

One of our speakers had not confirmed their times or speeches, so I was following up with them every couple of days. I was doing my best to check in sparingly, though I sent some of my messages at ten in the evening without thinking twice about the time of night.

One day, they blew up at me and threatened to not even come.

I'd not pushed anyone to this kind of anger for a long time, and I was not used to it. I don't know if it reminded me of when my mum used to blow up at me as a kid or what, but it triggered something in me and I bawled my eyes out for almost an hour.

I literally could not stop.

All the feelings I had bottled up for the last ten years exploded. The recent roller coaster with my dad, the feelings from speaking onstage, my mum's health, the pain and resentment I felt from my brothers... all of it and more came flowing through me at once and I screamed and cried in the fetal position for almost an hour.

As sad and as sickening as it felt, it was a needed release.

I don't blame the guy for snapping at me. We all go through tough times and say things we don't mean at times. It doesn't make us bad people, it just means we have bad days. There have been plenty of times I've wished people would just understand I am having a bad day and cut me some slack. Sadly, throughout my life, I got bad consequences for my outbursts, but I'm not going to mirror that onto everyone else.

The next few weeks were so stressful. The logistics of the live event were a nightmare, and I had no experience.

A friend of mine was also launching a new product the week of our event, and I wanted to top that leaderboard. In between printing and laminating name tags, I was sending emails and promos promoting the product and sleeping an average of three hours a night. I managed to top the leaderboard despite it having a fraction of my attention and won a MacBook Pro for coming in first place.

The MacBook Pro was a consolation prize compared to what I was really after: prestige. I wanted the screenshots and proof of my triumph over massive affiliates I could not have even dreamed of coming close to just months before. Not only did that give me a confidence boost and feeling of accomplishment, but it also gave me social clout I could use to help carry me to new heights.

Once you have social status and accomplishments of your own, it gets easier. The first six months online can be super brutal because you are starting from nothing, but once you get those screenshots of your name next to and above well-known superaffiliates, that is where the exponential growth comes.

My celebration was short-lived, however, as preparations for our event took over my life. From the moment I woke up to the moment I went to sleep, I worked like a madman to meet the deadlines and get the equipment sorted. I spent all my spare minutes printing out name tags and manually laminating table holders, as we had spent almost our entire budget on the venue itself.

On top of organizing the event, I was also one of its speakers. I was really proud of how I had performed at Brazil and Memphis the previous year and was ready to rock it once again. But it had been over four months since I spoke onstage last, and I had not really been around people much during this time. Confident speaking is not like riding a bike! If you don't use it, you lose it, and I could feel the nerves and hesitation creep back in. Plus, I had not prepared as much as usual for this speech because I was so busy planning the event.

My coorganizer, Michael, and I were both emceeing the event. Each time I got up to introduce someone, I felt the nerves and was hypercritical of myself for even the slightest pause or stutter.

It was a great event, and everyone loved it. I spoke to a few friends about how I wasn't happy with how I performed and the nerves I felt. They all told me I was being way too critical of myself and they hadn't even noticed: they thought I did a great job. This reinforced the fact that you always focus on your own mistakes far more and far longer than anyone else. In fact, most people don't even notice what you would call a mistake.

Although the event was awesome and everyone loved it, it wasn't successful financially. After everything was said and done, we actually lost money. I decided live events were not for me. I wanted to continue doing affiliate marketing, which was a breeze in comparison.

My business partner flew over from Canada to come and speak at our event, and while he was there, I reiterated my hatred of working on all of his pointless ideas that never amounted to anything. But he had me trapped and wasn't willing to let me go. Our Facebook groups had been created by him, all of our assets together were in his registered company address, and if I wanted to walk, I had to walk with nothing and risk breaking the terms of our signed agreement.

Ever since the altercation in January on the cruise, I had been searching for a way out.

In April 2019, the way out I was searching for came up.

He had been kicked out of the Builderall leadership for allegedly stealing leads, messaging people, and telling them to downgrade and then upgrade under him. When I spoke to him, I asked him outright if he had been doing it.

"If I find out you're lying to me," I said, "we are done." Turns out he had messaged hundreds of people, and we had all the recordings we needed to prove it.

He got kicked out of Builderall altogether, losing his account and all the commissions we had built together. I had been seeing a lawyer to learn how I could nullify our contract, and this was enough for a repudiatory breach of contract that nullified all our agreements.

I was finally free again.

I lost almost all of the assets we built together and had to restart my email list, Facebook group, and more. Thankfully, I was able to keep all of the leads and sales we had built together and merged our Builderall accounts.

That put me off partnerships for life and made me learn to be wary of signing documents! Luckily, it ended with minimal damages: it could have ended so much worse.

I was a free agent again and the world was my oyster. For the first time in my life, I truly looked forward to what lay ahead.

PART 4

SHAPING A LIFE I AM PROUD OF

CHAPTER 9

Getting Really Clear on What You Want

After I broke free from my ex–business partner, the next few months were some of the most carefree and enjoyable of my life. I started traveling again and became "homeless" by choice as I began to live the true nomad lifestyle.

I was invited back to Germany to speak at another Everest event. A few days later, I was back in Italy to speak in front of many of the people I had spoken in front of the year before for the first time. This time, I did a much better job, and instead of just speaking for fifteen minutes at a time, I was speaking for up to an hour at a time!

Shortly after that, I was back in the US for more marketing and personal development events. I got to stay in a mansion and was constantly around other people. My confidence was growing more and more, and I started to feel more at ease around others.

I was invited to a private yacht for a Mastermind event in Cancún, where I stayed at an all-inclusive five-star hotel that was paid for by the company. This was an invite-only event where you could not pay any amount of money to attend for high performers to network and help the company grow. This opened my eyes to how I could live if I kept on pushing forward. I was no longer content with just surviving: I wanted to thrive.

Despite earning tens of thousands a month, I still lived way below my means. If you want to catapult yourself fast, you need to do the same thing for a time. Don't upgrade your life to match your paycheck too fast!

What do I mean by that? Many people who get a bump in pay go out and spend it on unnecessary crap. "Ooh, I have an extra two grand a month coming in, so let's go rent a new apartment." "Ooh, a $500 bonus—I'll go buy some new clothes and treat myself. I've earned it!" That is not a good way to be.

Reinvest that money into your business until you *truly* have enough to spend. I am not saying to never treat yourself, but don't spend your money on unnecessary upgrades when you can survive with what you have.

Up until 2019, I had a 2002 Suzuki Swift 1.0. It was a terrible car. It took half a minute to get up to speed, had no power steering, and was so uninspiring to drive. It cost me £170 when I bought it—yes, $200 for a car that lasted almost two years! It was an incredibly good buy considering how long it lasted, but it was a cheap, horrible thing to drive!

I was still driving that car when I was making over $5,000 a month. I lived in an old, cold, moldy house until I was earning well over ten thousand a month. I could have easily gone and got a newer, warmer, more expensive place, but I could survive where I was. I still don't buy designer clothes and wear the same things I have had for years, because new flashy clothes are not a good investment.

There's a saying that whoever can hold their breath the longest wins. I held my breath for a long time before I started treating myself.

All the travels I went on and the events I attended were furthering my business. Every time I traveled, it was to a business event or conference, so it was an investment. When a company wasn't paying for my accommodation, I stayed in cheap Airbnbs or two-star hotels. There was the odd time I would treat myself, maybe to a nice car to drive in around the US, but that was usually because the front desk upsold me for an incredible deal.

Don't hold your breath until you can only barely afford something. You'll end up wasting that money when you could have invested it into something that would have leapfrogged your momentum!

Many people may disagree with me here and say, "Well why didn't you save any money?" Because I knew that in order to leapfrog forward, I had to invest in my business. I have chosen to spend *every* spare penny I have back into advertising, training, and growth on my business.

There are three main reasons I do this:

1. I don't have a massive tax bill at the end of the year because I am putting earnings back into my business. If I saved some of my income, I would have to pay taxes on it. Instead, I reinvest into the business until I make so much, I don't care about paying the taxes on it!

2. I skyrocket so much faster because I am getting more and more returns from the money I pour back into my business. Think about it. If I spent a thousand extra pounds a month on a nicer place for rent, that is a thousand pounds that doesn't go into my business.

Once I figured out ads, I knew I could just about break even the first month and profit the next month, so I spent every cent on ads, even if it meant running out of money every week and sometimes not knowing where I was going to sleep at night.

It may sound crazy, but running my ads was the most important thing to me, and I would often live like a pauper to make sure I spent the maximum amount I possibly could on them.

Because of that, I managed to build up tens of thousands of dollars in recurring income, which now keeps coming in every month, even when I turn my ads off completely.

3. I live frugally and refuse to surround myself with luxurious things, and it keeps me hungry and wanting more. If you're always surrounded by luxury and everything you want, you won't be so motivated to push forward.

A taste of luxury and indulgence is good as it gives you a sense of what is to come, but living in it before you can truly afford it is going to stop you from getting to the next level.

After a couple of weeks in Cancún, I went back to Florida for more events. I was attending or speaking at an event every couple of weeks at this time. My exponential growth and confidence boost were because of my complete immersion in my business.

A few months into my travels, I took a trip to New York that changed the whole trajectory of my journey.

I was happy with the way everything was going. I was earning tens of thousands of dollars doing next to no hours of work per week. I just logged into my ads account once a month to check they were still running and collect the recurring commissions I had built up over the last few years. This was the dream: complete and utter freedom to do what I wanted, where I wanted, how I wanted. All I had to do was travel around the world, attend dozens of events per year, share my story onstage, and only work a few hours a month.

Yet a chance meeting on an Uber ride into the city one day made me reevaluate my priorities.

I got an Uber ride to Manhattan, and the driver and I started talking about what I did and how I got there. And then we got into my backstory. He opened up to me and said *he* suffered sexual abuse as a child too and had been struggling with suicidal thoughts and depression in the last few months. We exchanged numbers, and the next day he messaged me.

What he said next shocked me: "Thank you so much for being so open with me; it was what prompted my honesty. I have never done that before."

"You never told your story to a stranger?" I replied.

"No, I'd never told anyone about that before."

I was stunned.

He had *never* told another living soul his entire life. He had carried that around with him for over twenty years until a random stranger opened up to him on a forty-five-minute Uber ride into the city.

That is the power of being vulnerable and sharing your story, the power of opening up and letting people know your struggles. Most people are going through similar things, but they never talk about them.

I thought about how painful it had been to hold in all my rage and sadness for so long. I remember the feeling of a great weight being lifted the first time I spoke about what had happened to me. The acceptance I felt let me know I wasn't alone and others had similar feelings. By sharing my story, I liberated myself from what I'd tried to keep hidden for so long. It was incredible to think that my story and vulnerability had such power to help people heal from their past traumas.

I imagined how many other people were struggling every day. How many people could I help by breaking the stigma around mental health and making it a less taboo subject to talk about?

In the beginning, sharing my story was a release for me. A way to heal. A way to not feel so alone and to know other people understood how I felt and related to me. Now, I saw the true power of sharing my story. My past struggles were becoming a superpower.

My whole life, I thought opening up and talking about my struggles made me weak. Yet it was the complete opposite. You never know how much you can help others who are scared to speak by stepping up first, being vulnerable, and sharing your story. We all have stories within us, whether we've been through hell or had it easy. Our own pain hurts, and it is up to us to choose whether we will use that pain for negative or positive purposes.

The message the Uber driver sent me that day stuck in my head and lit a fire under me to push back into high gear. There was no time to rest on my laurels and become satisfied with what I'd accomplished. It was time to get back to work. Before, my burning desire had just been to make something of myself. To prove to myself and everyone around me I was more than the layabout loser I had been ground into.

Now, I had a passion bigger than myself to work toward. I hadn't had a purpose for so long beyond existing. I now had a purpose for the first time in a decade, and it felt incredible.

I started speaking more frequently and putting myself out there even more. The fear subsided faster than ever, as it wasn't about me anymore. It was about helping others. I spoke at a high-level Mastermind group that caught the attention of a number of big players who loved my mission and wanted to help. I spoke on a cruise ship in the middle of the Bahamas and gained more traction. I was speaking and traveling, speaking and traveling, but didn't feel like I was having much impact. After my speeches, people would feel motivated for a while and some would take action and speak out. Yet there was something missing.

It was around this time that I met my first mentor. I was very self-reliant. I never asked for help and did everything on my own. Asking for help was always a sign of weakness in my eyes. It was quite impressive I managed to get as far as I did on my own, but tenacity, grinding, and obsession could only get me so far. I still had a lot to learn about asking for help and allowing others to take things off my plate, as I would so painfully learn soon enough.

I had traveled to New York to attend a small Mastermind event as part of an offer I had bought months prior. I turned up to a giant building in the heart of New York and went up to one of the top floors. I wandered to the reception desk and said I was there for the meeting.

The receptionist rang through and said, "Your appointment is here, Mr. Gold."

As he came through to greet me, he immediately said, "That is not my client."

I explained how I was there for the Mastermind event, and the email told me to come there on that day.

His face dropped as he told me the meeting had happened yesterday. An email had been sent out a couple of weeks ago changing the date to the day before, yet it had ended up in my spam box, so I didn't see it!

Instead of turning me away like most people would, Mr. Gold spent the entire day alone with me, teaching what he had taught to a group the day before.

Mr. Gold showed me that if I truly wanted to help people break through and live lives full of purpose, I would need to do more than just share my story and inspire people. I would need to take them to the next level too.

This was when we started working on my Massive Affiliate Blueprint product, the most comprehensive affiliate marketing training and program on the market today.

It was a tough transition.

Affiliate marketing is one of the easiest and simplest business models in the world. You do not need to deal with tech, product support, or fulfillment. If I had known the stresses of product creation, fulfillment, and customer support back then, I would have stuck to speaking and affiliate marketing full-time. Yet I am so glad I pivoted and built something that could truly help people: I have helped hundreds of my students generate millions of dollars in sales! Before these pivotal events, I was quite happy being a full-time marketer, traveling the world, speaking on stages occasionally, and living the life of a digital nomad.

It was that fateful cab ride in New York that prompted me to share my story more and want to help people who had been in my position, and it was Mr. Gold's intervention that showed me how sharing my story onstage was only a small part of what I could be doing to truly help people.

I now knew what I really wanted to do. I wanted to help people break free from the prisons of their own minds. I wanted to help people live with purpose and do things they could be proud of. I wanted to help people just like me do what I had done and bring them back from the brink of despair.

But I had a long road ahead of me.

At the end of our day together, I asked Mr. Gold why he had taken the time with me instead of turning me away. He spoke about the power of one, which brought me back to the lesson I had learned helping the lady in Germany who wanted to run offstage. If you take the time to help just one person, you don't know how many millions are going to be touched because of it.

It ignited a new purpose and passion in me to help as many people as I could. I especially wanted to help people who were in positions similar to mine a few short years back. I wanted to reach out to people who couldn't get jobs elsewhere because of their mental health conditions. I wanted to help them pull themselves up from the holes they had dug themselves into over the years. I wanted to show them a way to make a full-time living online, pull themselves up, sustain themselves, and become online entrepreneurs.

I wanted to create a place where people could come to follow their dreams. A place to be authentic and embrace self-expression without fear. A place where anyone could grow and where opportunity would be all around.

I made this my mission because I knew how hard it was to have no hope. I knew what it was like to not be able to function in a regular job. I knew what it was like to feel like there was no way out and no point in living. I knew what despair had driven me to. I knew how hard it was to believe I would never become anything, and I knew how helpful it was to have a helping hand. It was why I had such a burning desire to help.

So I started to get to work at the end of 2019 on my brand-new program—my Massive Affiliate Blueprint product—that was going to change the world! In January 2020, I did some more traveling and networking to let people know about my program, which I was aiming to launch in April. I went to four different events in the first six weeks of 2020 and then came back to the UK to work on my new product.

In my professional life, I had found focus and purpose. I knew exactly what I wanted, and I was willing to go after it. But my focus on work and traveling meant my health had been taking a back seat for a while—for a *long* while. I was putting on a lot of weight, sitting at a desk all day staring at a screen, and barely getting a thousand steps per day.

One day in 2020, I looked in the mirror and saw an unhealthy, 230-pound body staring back at me. I looked pregnant, my face was fat, and I was disgusted by what I saw. I wasn't going to allow myself to get any bigger.

I knew it was time to change.

So, in February 2020, I started a fitness program called Insanity and worked out intensely six days a week for eight weeks. Once again, I became clear on what I wanted: to finally be in a body that felt like my own.

CHAPTER 10

Pushing to the Edge of Mortality

I collapsed on the floor, sweat pouring off of me. Every fiber of my being hurt, and I thought my lungs were going to explode. As I lay there hearing my heart beat like a marching-band drum, I wondered if I would be able to go on.

And then my time was up. It was time to go again.

Insanity is arguably one of the hardest workout programs on the planet.

As you know by now, I don't do things halfway, and working out was no different. Every day, I would attack my Insanity workout with everything I had, collapsing in a pool of my own sweat at the end of every set...only to get up thirty seconds later and attack it again.

I legitimately didn't know a human could sweat that much and not die. There were days when every part of me, physically and mentally, wanted to just shut down. Yet, I was determined not to put on another pound. The sickening image of myself was burnt into my mind, and I wasn't going to let that be my reality.

You've got to be harsh with yourself if you want to make a change. I looked in the mirror and was disgusted by what I saw. If you kid yourself and try to make yourself feel better, you won't be motivated to change. Our minds are always trying to trick us into being comfortable. Your mind will try to make you believe everything is fine and justify why you are the way you are:

I've been working really hard, so I deserve to eat junk food.

I'm focusing on work; I will exercise later.

Insert excuse here, concession here. We constantly try to justify things to make ourselves feel better about our own choices, but it's in these moments of denial we deny ourselves the opportunity for growth. It's in the moments of discomfort and pain we can become better versions of ourselves. If you want it bad enough, you will be able to push yourself to levels that once seemed unfathomable to you.

Before 2017, I would physically push myself to about 10 percent of my capacity and stop. I was weak and moved away from pain and discomfort as much as possible. Similar to pushing through fear, when you begin to push through bodily pain and discomfort, you will see exponential results much faster.

So I kept going and pushed through as much as I could, despite wanting to stop.

Persistence is what separates the strong from the weak. Persistence is where the real magic happens and where you start achieving the results you want to see. There were days my legs wanted to snap and I couldn't do as much, but I didn't skip a day. I didn't stop.

If you show up every day and stay in it, then you can give it your all. But the *most* important thing is simply showing up to do the work. The one thing that kept me going was just getting myself to press play on the workout video. I made the commitment to just press play and do my best. It would have been easy to say, "I am skipping today because I can barely stand up, let alone work out," but with one concession comes another and another.

Tell me if this sounds familiar:

You're on a diet or a workout plan. You're doing really well, sticking to everything like a champ, and then one day, you have a moment of weakness. You skip a day, eat a piece of cake, or do something that seems like a small slipup, and that break in discipline and consistency messes everything up. Suddenly, you're snacking between meals and missing workouts frequently, and you just give up entirely.

All it takes is that one moment of weakness for you to completely lose motivation and start bending the rules even further.

However, if you mess up and miss a day or break your diet, it's not the end of the world. Many people will use it as an excuse to fall back into old habits and say they "failed." This is just an excuse to quit and fall back into comfort. A bad day is just a bad day, and you need to focus on each individual day instead of looking too far ahead.

Whether it's a huge work project, a diet plan, or an exercise regime, stop getting overwhelmed by the distant future! Don't focus on next month or next week. Heck, don't even focus on tomorrow. We aren't guaranteed tomorrow. Worry about today only.

I don't know what I am going to eat a week from now, how I am going to feel, or if I'm even going to be here! What I know is today...

I am going to do my exercises today...

I am going to eat right today...

I am going to write one page for my book today...

I will put my all into my project today...

I can't say I will tomorrow, but I know I will today.

I'm not saying not to plan. You should and must plan for some things. But don't focus on the whole process of a difficult task, and don't count the cost of the cumulative effort involved over weeks or months. It will just demotivate you. Focus on today and live in the now, and you will be amazed at how much more productive you are.

During my Insanity program, I was eating one meal a day with a shake for breakfast, and when I wasn't working out, I was spending every waking hour building my new program. Hour after hour, day after day, and week after week, I worked like crazy, commonly going to bed after sunrise and waking up at midday. I was obsessed and lacked the capacity to trust anything to anyone else. I did pretty much everything alone.

I had hired a couple of virtual assistants from the Philippines to help with my day-to-day tasks, but I was terrible at business and management. I had learned to be an amazing marketer, but running a business and managing employees was alien to me. They would post incorrect content in my online groups and follow instructions poorly. I ended up paying them for doing nothing most of the time.

The bulk of everything fell squarely on me. I figured out the tech, the automations, and the sales pages. I created and wrote the webinar and all the emails. I created the images, the integrations, the videos, the scripts, and the editing. My coach helped and guided me on the planning for my product and launch, but I did the implementation myself. To my detriment, I did it all.

I was always in max gear on something. For years it was my business: I never slowed down, and my health and relationships took a hit because of it. When I went all in on my health, I went into max gear doing Insanity until I literally collapsed on the floor, and then I stood back up to do it again. I lost thirty-three pounds in a matter of weeks and continued to go all in on my business again.

April 2020 came and went, and I kept pushing myself. The worldwide COVID-19 lockdown had no effect on me: my entire life was waking up, working out, sitting behind a computer, and repeating seven days a week.

After the actual product was finished, I realized the launch of the product was going to be its own beast. I had not anticipated everything that went into a huge joint venture launch, and we had now set a hard date for October 15.

As the date got closer and closer, the hours got longer and longer.

I was often getting two to four hours of sleep before waking up and powering through the next day. An extremely unhealthy amount of caffeine and overworking were pushing me to my very limit. During the launch period, there was one crisis after another. I had a mental breakdown and burst into tears multiple times. Despite my past, I believe these were some of the most stressful months of my life.

I had been aiming for a million-dollar launch, which was a very lofty goal. Very few vendors ever do a million-dollar launch, and I was aiming for it my first time!

Only a very small percent of people ever do million-dollar launches and I was aiming for one on my *first* ever launch.

In the two-week launch period, we sold $350,000, only a third of my target. We had a number of tech issues and scheduling issues, which I know lost us a lot of sales.

Not long after the launch, I was speaking to my friend Omar and telling him how it had gone, and I remember the words he said to me exactly:

"Okay, hold on. You did $350,000 on your first-ever launch and you are beating yourself up about it? Dude, that is amazing! Our first launch got *zero* sales. To do a multi-six-figure launch your first time is amazing."

He was right. I set myself an unrealistic goal, and it bummed me out when I didn't achieve it.

You've got to detach yourself from the outcome. If you're too attached to it, fear can easily creep in and cloud your judgment. It can paralyze you and prevent you from taking action, or it can kill your drive if you don't get the result you're attached to.

Don't get me wrong: you need to set lofty goals to keep yourself excited and moving forward. If I had only set $100,000 as the goal, would I have done $350,000? Probably not. However, you need to not be so attached to that lofty goal that it seriously demotivates you if you don't hit it.

After the launch, the product fulfillment stresses began, which I again had vastly underestimated. Support tickets were coming in by the dozens each day, things were breaking, and fixes were needed in addition to all the calls and workshops I had promised.

On top of this, my two virtual assistants were getting worse by the month, and I found out they were doing less than what I was paying them for. When I finally fired them, I locked them out of everything they had been granted access to—except I forgot one thing: the checkout inside Builderall with all my payment processors.

The day I fired them, they changed all of my payment processors to their PayPal and siphoned thousands of dollars to their account. Luckily, I noticed the very next day, and Builderall got on the ball reversing all of the charges.

My team was gone and tasks were piling up by the dozen. Luckily, a couple of my friends offered to help, and I ended up hiring two trustworthy people to replace my virtual assistants, one of whom was Randy Rowell. This new team took some of the pressure off, but there was still so much to do.

Finally, the stress of working eighteen-hour days for close to a year made itself felt. In December, I ended up in the hospital multiple times. I had pushed myself way too hard for way too long. All the stresses I had put my body through and the constant mental effort all came together, and I was incapacitated.

There are countless entrepreneurs who push themselves to the nth degree and suffer serious health consequences for the rest of their lives because of it. I am sure the damage I caused myself took at least a few years off my life, but I got off easy compared to many. This was my body's early warning sign to stop and slow down, and unlike many other people, I listened to it.

I gradually started handing over the reins.

Randy Rowell was an incredible hire. I had truly found a diamond in the rough to help bring my dreams to reality. He was an absolute superstar who would work on my business day and night. It's hard to find people who are not just in it for themselves and who are willing to help bring your dream and vision to life. There wasn't a bad bone in his body, and you could tell he had good principles and was a down-to-earth, honest guy. He truly believed in what I was creating and was very attached to bringing my programs to the masses to help people.

No matter how many times you are betrayed, stabbed in the back, kicked when you are down, and lied to, you can't give up hope. You can't let the actions of a few bad apples discolor your views on the rest of the world. I did that for a long time, and it almost killed me. There are many more nice people in the world than nasty. Unfortunately, the nasty ones seem to be a lot louder and prominent than the nice ones!

Don't shut yourself off from everyone or turn down help from the right people because of your past sour experiences.

After enduring all of that and pushing myself to the brink of my own mortality, I came to realize that nothing is worth losing my health over. If a job needs doing, it can be done on work time: I will never push myself past midnight for anyone or anything again. Above all else, you need to look after yourself. If you find you have nothing left to give, then you are doing people a disservice by pushing yourself too far.

It was a rough couple of months as I learned these lessons.

While I wasn't able to work, I had a lot of time to reflect. The goal had always been freedom, and although my programs were helping a lot of people and had given me a very high-paying job, they had taken away my own freedom.

I thought about closing it all down and throwing in the towel. I was happier just doing affiliate marketing and speaking, anyway. I would have fewer worries and stresses, and most importantly, I would have freedom.

I was earning tens of thousands a month in recurring commissions from my affiliate marketing efforts with zero hours of work, so I could have easily shut everything down and stepped back. But my conscience would not let me do that. There were hundreds of people who had invested their time and money in me, and as much as I wanted my freedom back, I couldn't let everyone down.

Something had to change, though. I couldn't keep doing the same thing.

CHAPTER 11

Balance, Rest, and Difficult Success

I had just spent the last year and a half creating a *lot* of different things. Since my change of direction in New York, I had made it my mission to help as many people as I could who were suffering in silence like I had for so many years.

This included sharing my story and speaking onstage as much as possible, as well as building an empire of all the things that would help people make something of themselves online. I created small pieces of software for lead generation, affiliate marketing training, done-for-you systems, one-click rebrandable reports and lead magnets, membership areas, Private Label Rights products, and more.

Having not launched my own programs before, I didn't know how much support and fulfillment was going to take out of me. The launch itself was the most stressful few weeks of my life and almost broke me. Luckily, the fulfillment and support efforts were nowhere near as stressful, but they still required a lot of time, energy, and effort from me.

It was a massive "grow or die" moment for me, and I was forced to work like crazy again to simplify everything. I had no systems, processes, or structure in place, and I had done it all myself, so there was no one who understood the systems I had created or could help me fix or edit them! This meant if anything broke in the system or any bugs needed fixing, I was the only one with the answers.

I had also built most of my programs on third-party software, so if something technical went wrong or they added a feature that broke one of my automations, I had to rely on their development team to make the fix.

It was then I realized I was doing everything all wrong.

Instead of building dozens of different programs and systems and doing everything for everyone, I needed to stick to a few core products I could deliver on really well.

More is not always better.

You see, if you stretch yourself too thin too fast, you dilute the quality of everything you do. Sure, you can build an empire of digital products and services, but it doesn't happen overnight, and if you rush it, you will inevitably implode.

My initial thought was to build an empire of "all the things." I would be able to help everyone with everything they needed, and it would be awesome! I learned the hard way that it didn't quite work like that. I couldn't support, fix, fulfill, and grow all of the programs at once, and as a result, they all suffered.

So I began systematically simplifying everything and getting rid of the dead weight to trim down the monstrous number of things I had created. Once I started focusing on just three of my core products instead of dozens, I found I was helping more people and earning more in the process.

Just after my launch, I began working with a now close friend of mine, Dan Meredith. Dan is a very successful entrepreneur, and I had been following him since 2017 when I first got started. I always related to his values, sense of humor, and character. I admired how he was unapologetically himself while building a seven-figure business and didn't care what others thought of him, which was something I still struggled with.

We originally began to work together at the end of 2020 for the purpose of planning my book. Again, I seriously underestimated the commitment and fulfillment of the beast I had just launched and wanted to get started on my book right away.

The health issues I experienced in December changed those plans drastically. I couldn't keep pushing in sixth gear all the time on my business; I needed to find some sort of balance.

Balance has never been a thing in my life. For many years, I didn't try at anything and sat on the sidelines, never putting in any effort. Yet 2017 flicked the switch. Suddenly, everything was always all or nothing, all in or all out. No middle ground, no half-assing anything. I had that drilled into me from a young age: if you're going to try at something, give it everything you've got.

Although that worked for me in many regards, it badly hurt me in many others. Hence the myriad of health issues I was experiencing. There is such a thing as a healthy obsession, but my obsessions were never healthy: they consumed my entire life, and anything I wasn't fixated on got neglected.

Sleep had been a problem for years. I had taken melatonin on and off since I was seven, but the problems hadn't ever disappeared. I would frequently spend two to four hours lying in bed before falling asleep.

This was a huge reason why my sleep patterns were so erratic. I hated losing time and productivity, so I would work until I passed out at six in the morning. Otherwise, I felt like I was wasting an hour or two a day trying to get to sleep.

Dan recommended a call with someone he had used for sleep coaching: Angus Buckle. In the past, I struggled to take advice from anyone and never wanted anyone's actions to influence mine. I always wanted my changes to come from myself and to have complete ownership of everything.

However, health challenges forced me to change my ways.

Sleep is a foundational aspect of our health, and if you aren't getting enough high-quality sleep, it will affect everything you do. I could write an entire book about what I learned from Angus about sleep, but I would be doing a disservice to the topic if I touched on it here.

I always looked at life as having three overarching focuses: health, wealth, and relationships. I had the habit of going into max gear pursuing wealth to the detriment of the others. I had a one-track mind and would turn the computer on instantly upon waking and get to work. I had no notable relationships to speak of, and my health had taken a dive as well because of my obsession to work.

It was a difficult transition toward balance and one I still struggle with today, yet I am light-years ahead of where I was at the beginning of 2020. Life is a continuous journey of growth and bettering oneself. It never ends, and the moment you think you know it all is the moment your downfall will begin.

If you're not growing, you're dying.

So at the start of 2021, I began following Angus's advice.

I originally started working with him just for sleep, but he helped me with so much more. I developed a morning routine, something I had never done before. The first hour of the day was mine. I would wake up, drink a liter of water, jump in a cold shower, walk the dog while listening to Les Brown, do ten minutes of stretches, make coffee, and *then* turn the computer on.

Before, I would just wake up, put the kettle on, and go to work.

This simple morning routine stuck with me and made a major difference in my mood and productivity. Instead of waking up to a barrage of messages, emails, support tickets, and fires to put out, I spent the first hour completely disconnected.

Some light exercise and insights from some of the world's greatest speakers on a morning walk helped me experience more growth and creativity during a time I was constantly fixing things and doing the same mundane tasks every day to fulfill my promises on my product.

The first hour or two after you wake up is so important. If the first thing you do in the morning is check your phone and lose yourself in social media, I implore you to stop. You are allowing other people and potential negative energy into your life at your most impressionable time. By simply taking the first hour or two to yourself each day, you can control the narrative of your own life and learn to be proactive instead of reactive.

After just a few weeks of changing some foundational habits, I could notice a difference. I also developed an evening routine, which was as important as the morning routine. Having a hard cut-off time for work allowed me to have a couple of hours of fun in the evenings before cutting off from screens entirely an hour before bed.

It's important to reiterate that I had struggled with sleep problems since I was seven years old. I thought I had tried absolutely everything and that I was just doomed to a life of crappy sleep. Yet within three months of working with Angus, I saw a massive improvement in the duration and quality of my sleep. I was even falling asleep faster, which was a huge win.

Over the next six months of working with Dan and Angus, I started to see all areas of my life get better. It didn't happen overnight, and it took a lot of discipline to stick to it all, but I wanted it badly enough that the discipline came easily.

Discipline and consistency are now the two most important things in life. I used to buck off anything that looked like routine. I had the most rebellious attitude growing up and hated conforming and doing as I was told. Yet once I started imposing self-discipline, got really clear on what I wanted, and became consistent with my routine and work ethic, everything changed for the better.

Small, consistent actions lead to the greatest results. It's not exciting —in fact, it's boring—but what's exciting is the end result and the accomplishment you feel once you've achieved your goal.

I scaled back my workouts by scheduling them for just twice a week. Previously, I would go on crazy workout schedules and push myself to the breaking point. Remember Insanity? Here's an example of how bad it got: six weeks into the program, I seriously injured my back. Instead of quitting and allowing it to heal, I did something really stupid. I started eating painkillers every day and just pushed through the last two weeks, messing my back up even worse. It contributed to my health breakdown in December.

In short, I pushed myself to the edge, always—my exercise was not consistent, and I couldn't sustain it indefinitely. Thanks to Angus, I had a routine of just two tough workouts per week with enough time to recover and grow in between.

Sunday became a rest day where I did nothing strenuous or anything remotely resembling work. I often spent these days with Mum or my brothers.

This, of course, had been a major weak area before, as all my time was spent on the business and not on building relationships with those close to me. My family got along a lot better now, and we had all apologized and made amends for the way we treated one another growing up. But the bonds were not yet strong. Investing time into those relationships was important and made all the difference.

For the first time in my life, I felt balance and had an energy other than the pure drive and determination that had been propelling me for so long. I realized I could experience more balance and growth in my health, wealth, *and* relationships instead of becoming obsessed with one at a time while the others suffered.

I was starting to enjoy my best health ever, and my business and relationships were on the up and up too!

If you're worried it's too late for you and you will never be able to find balance, then let me assure you that it's possible for everyone. You're never too far down the road or too old; you just have to start. Change is always within your grasp.

Let me give you the example of my mum. Around the same time I was getting my life back into balance, I started helping her get her own health back. For the last four years, she had been in and out of the hospital with infections and four bouts of sepsis, one of which she barely survived.

As I mentioned before, in 2017, she had stepped on a tack that went into her foot and caused an infection. For most people, this would not have been an issue, but Mum was diabetic and had poor circulation. The complications from the wound sent her into a deep depression, made worse by the fact she had recently lost her house.

The healthcare service and many of the professionals she saw were less than adequate. Many doctors in her hospital wanted to cut both her feet off. The doctors stopped her from walking for months on end and her foot became crooked because of it. They refused her physical therapy because all they wanted to do was take her feet off.

As soon as I was able, I took matters into my own hands and paid for weekly physical therapy myself. I bought the best rehab exercise equipment for her to help regain her strength. We started going out together and doing fun things to cheer her up. Mum literally had not been out of the house in a year except for hospital visits and really did not want to go anywhere to begin with.

The first time we went out, we went for a drive to Sandringham, a forest we frequented when I was a child before everything got messed up. I don't know what it was, but from that day on, she seemed to change. She had more motivation, and a fire that had been extinguished for a few years began to grow.

Sunday became our day to visit forests, beaches, spas, resorts, and more.

Slowly, a desire to get better and hope for the future was returning.

It's a beautiful thing when you can inspire someone who has given up hope to try again, and even more so when that person is your own mother. Thanks to what I had achieved in the past few years and the therapy and equipment I could afford thanks to my newfound income, my mum gained new motivation and worked hard to get better.

Today, Mum is out of the wheelchair and training to become a certified psychotherapist and coach—in her fifties! Another true testament to the fact it's never too late to find purpose and achieve success.

By May 2021, most of the fulfillment for my new product was done, and I was paying out over $50,000 per month in commissions to my students from my products alone. Things were ticking along nicely, and I could finally ease off the pedal.

It was the perfect opportunity to take some time off.

I always feel bad taking time off. I see all my students asking questions in the group and my team working, and I feel like I should be working too.

Any decent entrepreneur feels like this while they're growing and outsourcing: you have put in the time, energy, and effort to get to this point. But if you truly want to get to the next level, you need to let it go, not micromanage, and release your grip on the reins. If you don't, you will become the bottleneck in your own business, and your team and customers will suffer as a result.

The thing I most struggle with is that there is always something else to be done. I can tweak a headline here, add a bonus there, split-test something else, add a new upsell, answer someone's question, or make another call. The list of things I *can* do is endless, and as an entrepreneur, it can be very hard to have an off switch as there's no one telling me when and how to work.

This same switch can be hard to turn *on* for many people for the same reason. Many would-be entrepreneurs figure, *With no boss to tell me what to do, why don't I just go and watch TV?* Constantly being switched on helped me grow as fast and soar as high as I did. However, it was also the thing grinding me into the dirt and taking years off my life.

In the beginning, you should go all in and focus on success above all else. It's that healthy obsession that gets you off the ground. You may say, "James, I have kids, I work, and I don't get a minute to myself all day."

Okay, then: it may take you longer than someone who has twelve hours a day to dedicate to their business, but with enough determination, you can carve out an hour or two a day to devote to your dream.

If you want it badly enough, you will give up social time, TV time, game time, and even a few hours of sleep a night if that's what it takes. During my launch, I slept about three hours a night for weeks, so there are no excuses. Just remember to slow down and take your foot off the pedal when you get some traction so you don't work your way into an early grave like I almost did.

In order to succeed like I did, you need to be willing to sacrifice the present for the future. You need to be willing to spend a few years in a way most people won't so you can spend the rest of your life in a way most people can't. That means going all in.

No dabbling. No half-assed attempts for a few hours a week.

All in with every spare moment you have.

When you reach a certain level, you can start delegating to others and ease off the pedal a bit, but those first six months or more, you need to be committed. It is so worth it when you unlock a freedom most only dream of.

Now that things were finally ticking along without much input from me, Dan invited me down to spend some time with him in Devon. I lived in Cambridgeshire on the other side of the country, and it was a four-hour drive from my place to Devon.

On one of the first days down there, we were walking along the beach talking about things, and I got onto the topic of confidence. Despite regularly speaking onstage in front of thousands of people at this point, I still found it difficult to hold conversations and lacked confidence around new people.

Dan took one look at me and said, "You can't expect to be confident if you don't look the part. For fuck's sake, you're a seven-figure marketer and you look like a fucking pikey—go buy some new clothes."

Now, the old me would have taken major offense and told him to go fuck himself. The new me was always open to taking constructive criticism however it was delivered, especially from someone I looked up to and wanted to emulate.

Still slightly offended, though, I replied, "This is my best top; it's nice."

"No, no it's not."

He was right. I still lived way below my means, driving a fifteen-year-old car and wearing tracksuits and five-year-old clothes. Like I said, they weren't important investments to me and I could survive with the things I had, so why spend on unnecessary crap?

Again, this was a great mindset to get me to where I was. But as always, I had taken it too far by living like a pauper to keep reinvesting in my business and neglecting myself.

It was time to flip another switch.

I slowed my ads and started treating myself and my family more. The next week, I took my mum for a week away down in Devon. She had the best time. It was so nice to see happiness and hope in her eyes again and to know she was enjoying life despite still being in a wheelchair at the time.

While we were in Devon, I surprised Mum with a real treat. She hadn't been able to walk, run, cycle, or feel the wind in her hair for over four years at this point. So one day, we went hang gliding for the first time!

It was a struggle to get off the ground as we were supposed to run in order to get airborne. Yet thanks to the stellar staff and service at Fly like a Bird in Devon, we made it happen!

During these trips to Devon, I spent zero time on my business and still generated over $70,000 while I was off hang gliding, surfing, and vacationing. This is the beauty of having an online business that works for you long after you've put in the initial work.

After we returned from Devon, I hired Angus to also coach Mum on sleep, fitness, healthy living, and everything that had helped me get into my best health ever over the last six months. And as you already know, my mum made a full recovery and is on her way to becoming a psychotherapist.

Her story also demonstrates the "power of one" that Mr. Gold taught me. I'd been focusing on my health for a while now, but nothing I did encouraged my brothers to do the same. But after witnessing my mum's transformation and dedication to her health, my brothers also started dieting and working out more. She inspired them.

You never know what kind of domino effect you are having on people around you. You can be a shining ray of hope and inspiration for everyone.

Around this time, I also bought Mum her dream car. Ever since she was seventeen, she had dreamed of owning a red Mercedes convertible.

The look of surprise and then joy on her face that day is something I will never forget.

For five years, she had been depressed, feeling lower and lower with each year. She had been in and out of the hospital, falling deeper and deeper into isolation and hopelessness. Yet in 2021, everything changed. The hang gliding and the car ticked off two bucket list items in as many weeks, and my mum got a new lease on life and a desire to try again.

The next few months, Randy, the team, and I prepared to relaunch my Rapid Profit Machine (RPM) program.

My RPM was a smaller version of my Massive Affiliate Blueprint program. It was designed to let complete newbies to affiliate marketing get their foot in the door. It teaches the basics of affiliate marketing, traffic, and the nature of the business.

Despite some setbacks, we had a successful launch in August 2021 and I was ready to take another break. I hadn't traveled abroad since before the lockdown in February 2020, and I was itching to start exploring again. I had three people working for me at this point, so I handed over the day-to-day activities to them.

I traveled to Mexico, Texas, Florida, California, and Nevada over the next three months, visiting dozens of different cities and having an amazing time.

Unfortunately, in October, I caught COVID, and it messed me up badly. I felt like I was going to die for three days, and if it weren't for the prospect of a $20,000 medical bill and the thought of being put on a ventilator, I would have probably called the emergency services.

Instead, I just stuck it out and stayed in bed, going from hot to cold and sleeping on and off.

Each cough felt like a knife cutting through my lungs, and I was forced to breathe shallowly to stop myself from coughing and doing any further damage. My smell and taste were completely gone. I could swill apple cider vinegar and taste nothing. To make matters worse, I had pulled my back badly from overtraining (again), so I was in constant pain and found it hard to walk.

I felt the effects of COVID for six months and only regained my taste, smell, and the ability to think clearly and push myself hard in workouts in March of 2022. Vitamin IV and NAD+ therapy helped me bounce back in the short term, and I had more than enough energy to thoroughly enjoy my time in the US.

At the beginning of 2020, I had purchased a package from my friends Omar and Melinda Martin to work on my business at their house in Florida. Due to circumstances, we couldn't do it as planned in 2020 and instead of doing it virtually, I opted to postpone it until time allowed.

In November 2021, we went ahead with it.

Omar and Melinda had been prepping for this beforehand by interviewing me, and I had told them I needed the most help with putting together a great roadmap. One night as we were chatting, however, I explained my current situation, and they came to the conclusion that I needed something else entirely.

Structurally, my business was a complete mess.

My entire business was in my head. I was grossly overpaying people for simple tasks. I had no standard operating procedures, and everything was a muddled mess. No one had any direction, and I responded reactively to everything.

This had worked to get me to where I was and achieve so much so fast, but it was no way to run a seven-figure business. I always rushed ahead with plans and never put any instructions in place so someone could come along and pick up the slack. I didn't take the time to train anyone on how I did things because I knew I could get things done ten times faster myself.

Not a great way to do things if you want to delegate as much as possible!

That night, Omar and Melinda discussed the possibility of working with me to sort my business out. The next morning, they came back to me with a proposal, and without hesitation, I said yes. I am a brilliant marketer, copywriter, technical wizard, and web page builder, but when it comes to the business side of things—structure, systems, processes, and planning—I suck!

I truly believe divine intervention brought us to that moment right there.

Back in 2020, when I couldn't do the package with them, I had been upset: I thought it would have been beneficial before my big launch.

But it could not have happened at a better time than right now, as the next few months would soon prove.

If something "goes wrong" or doesn't go as you expected, don't get upset. It's all part of the process, and most likely, it is setting you up for something greater down the line if you don't let it derail you.

While in the US, I visited and stayed with my team member Randy for a few weeks and had a blast. I met his wife, Belinda, was invited to Thanksgiving dinner with his family, went to a couple of events with him, and then we had some downtime in Las Vegas together.

Sadly, tensions had been mounting between two of my other team members, and during my trip in the US, it was becoming painfully obvious one of them had to go. I trusted them both implicitly, so it was surprising and painful for me to know one of them was manipulating others and lying to me.

In December, I had the proof I needed to let one of them go and was prepared for the rest of the team to pick up the slack. Be very careful whom you trust and let into your circle, and be especially wary of anyone who offers to help you for free: they usually have an ulterior motive.

With this person gone, I knew we would have an uphill battle to keep the business running smoothly. But nothing prepared me for what was to come.

On the twentieth of December, tragedy hit.

Randy was hospitalized after struggling with a bad case of COVID. He fought for a month in the hospital before I got the news from his wife near the end of January. He couldn't make it—he'd passed away.

I was devastated.

I lost a dear friend and two-thirds of my team in two weeks.

Randy did an awful lot for my business, and losing him and the other member of the team was catastrophic. On top of that, some of our systems had been failing us, and it was becoming apparent I was going to have to rebuild a large part of my business.

I'd just lost two of the people I spoke to more than anyone on a daily basis. Everything started to get to me, and I felt myself sliding into a bit of a depression. I was fighting with my old enemy anxiety again, and I could feel my motivation draining with each passing day.

The monumental tasks of rebuilding everything, fixing the issues that had been piling up, and getting everything running smoothly again with a new team felt insurmountable. I knew how much effort it took to build everything the first time. I didn't want to get up in the morning, and whenever I thought about doing anything, I would get pains in my chest.

Uncertainty and stress are terrible things, and if you can find a way to lower either of them, you will be a much happier human. At the beginning of 2022, Melinda went above and beyond to ensure I stayed afloat. I honestly think I may have reached my breaking point if we had not started working together back in November. Without her, the struggle would have been ten times greater.

Even with her, there was a mountain of things to be done. Moving checkouts, moving other services, hiring, retraining, integrations, migrations, tech headaches...the list goes on.

But I decided to focus on *one* thing at a time and chunk it down into manageable, bite-size pieces. Day by day, as the puzzle came together, the anxiety subsided and the steps seemed more manageable.

You see, the worst thing you can do when there's so much stress is stop. Freezing due to fear, stress, or lack of direction will only bring you more trouble and ensure you stay stuck in analysis paralysis.

It's been a challenge, but challenges only make us stronger if we can overcome them. There are always going to be challenges and struggles, no matter what level you are at. In fact, the more successful you become, the bigger the challenges become. With new levels come new devils. No matter how successful you are, there are always going to be frustrations and struggles. We're all human, and we all slip up all the time.

Plus, the more you have, the more people will try to worm their way in and take what you have worked so hard to build. Yet you can't allow that to stop you from trusting the right people. When the crap hit the fan in December, I could have crumpled and shut everyone out. But I didn't, and it made all the difference.

Many people who have followed me from the start have seen my up-and-down journey as an entrepreneur. The worst thing you can do when something goes wrong is try to cover it up and give it the big I am by acting overly important. One of the biggest things that helps me come back stronger is sharing my struggles to inspire people instead of hiding them and acting like everything is perfect.

I own the mess, get back up, and attack it.

Because it isn't all sunshine and rainbows.

Building a business takes time.

Building a long-lasting, successful business takes dedication.

If you try to act as if everything is a walk in the park and everything is perfect when things are falling apart, you will alienate everyone, losing their trust or completely demotivating them because "it's so easy for you" and not for them.

You'll create a false sense of reality that people strive for but are never able to attain.

You may think sharing the downs make you look weak. However, if you share everything, including the bad, the ugly, and the hardships, you build rapport with people and help them carry on when they are struggling themselves. It can be scary, and some people may troll you, but these people are sad lowlifes themselves who will never amount to anything without a mindset shift.

As I write these words, I find myself reflecting on this year. The year 2022 has been a very challenging year for me so far, but I have come out stronger on the other side. I'm happy to report that I now have an awesome, trustworthy team and the structures in place for someone to come in and pick up the slack if anything does happen.

Even when most things are going well, it can be a constant battle to maintain happiness, which is not a destination but an experience that comes and goes. One day, I will be on top of the world, enjoying every moment, and the next, my whole life will feel torn apart.

We cannot control the things that happen to us, but we can control how we react to them. Stressing over things we can't control just brings more stress and a lower life span. We need to appreciate the small things and feel happiness and gratitude each day.

If you anchor your emotions to success, you will never be truly happy.

Yes, I know this is cliché, but I'll say it again: happiness *is* a journey and not a destination. You need to find happiness in the everyday moments and not in lofty goals you have set for yourself.

If you do, you will find hitting that goal will not bring you lasting happiness at all, and you will be unfulfilled, unhappy, and unsatisfied, without a clue how to find true happiness.

Conclusion

Pouring from a Full Cup

If you had asked me in 2016 whether or not I believed I would some-day own a seven-figure business, I would have laughed at you. My life had been so difficult until then, its challenges seemed unsurmount-able. All I could do—all I knew how to do—was sit and play video games all day. I knew how to survive, but that was it.

The thought of ever thriving felt like a distant dream.

This is why I share my story with you today. My hope is that it will inspire you, uplift you, help you make changes, and empower you to keep going. As the Uber driver showed me during that cab ride, there is power in expressing our story and sharing all of our-selves, even the ugly bits. It may take courage, but the results are worth it.

Your life can change. I know it. I've lived that change.

Since I became the number one affiliate in the world for Builderall, many big players have reached out to me, wanting me to switch to their platforms and join them. Some have offered to rebuild everything I have in their platform for the switch, and some have offered me free lifetime access for the switch.

I even had the owner of one platform try to bribe me to join them!

But you couldn't pay me any amount of money to make the switch.

Builderall is where I got my start and where my closest friends are. The community members are the ones who were there for me through my initial growth, struggles, and confidence-building from the bottom.

When I was first getting started, Erick showed me grace for a few stupid mistakes I made, and I will never forget that.

One of the worst mistakes was during an affiliate competition back in 2018. For this launch, I had set up a joint venture page and added it on a big site that the product creator usually set up pages on. I thought it was a great way to get lots of sales and joint venture partners on board for the launch.

During the launch, I sent out a load of emails to affiliates who thought they were signing up on Builderall's page—but it was mine. Erick, the CEO of Builderall, got bombarded with complaints from affiliates that I was "spamming" them.

A huge thread ensued on Facebook with dozens of people calling for me to be banned.

Instead of kicking me to the curb, Erick listened to me and saw it was a genuine mistake. He took a hit from a number of big, well-known affiliates by refusing to ban me, and I have never forgotten the grace he showed me that day.

I could be a terror in my former life, and I still live with the regret of some things I did. I don't like the way it feels. I've suffered through many sleepless nights of regretting my actions and moments of weakness.

Loyalty and honor are always worth more than money. Erick and the Builderall community have been a huge part of my growth, and without Erick's support and guidance, I know I would not be where I am today.

I believe it's very important to give back and remember who supported you to get to where you are.

Yet, when you first begin, you need to look after yourself first.

I'm sure you've heard of the phrase, "Fit your own mask first." Before a plane takes off, the crew always instructs the passengers to fit their own oxygen masks before assisting others in an emergency. This is because you are of no use to someone else if you can't look after yourself first.

This lesson is as important in business as it is in life.

You need to look after your own interests first before anyone else's.

I know that sounds a bit harsh, but it is true, and you are doing yourself and everyone around you a disservice if you try to help before you get your own stuff together. I couldn't have helped my mum with her troubles and health if I hadn't gotten my act together first—I wouldn't have known Angus or had the money to pay for her treatment.

It's the same with business. You need to be selfish with your time and assets in the beginning to enable you to build up more. Only when you have plenty to give should you start giving, because if your cup is almost empty, then you won't be able to have such an impact.

What is the point of making your first $10,000, only to give it away and be left with nothing? It makes no sense when you can use that ten thousand to make one hundred thousand, and that one hundred thousand to make a million.

You could give $100,000 away once you've made a million and still have 90 percent of the million to do with as you please. You can give ten times more away and still have loads to continue to build on, which in turn enables you to give far more away down the line and have a far greater impact.

I am not saying to never be philanthropic. I have raised tens of thousands for charities with my programs and launches and plan to do a whole lot more, but if I had given to charity too soon, I would have shot myself and the charities in the foot because I would never have been able to give as much as I can now.

With that said, I am in a great position to give back now, and that is what I have been doing and will continue to do. Thanks to my online programs, hundreds of my students have cumulatively generated millions of dollars, and with the way things are going, that number will be a hundred times greater in the near future. The people I have impacted can then go on to create their own programs and do great things to have an even larger impact on the world.

As Mr. Gold taught me with the power of one, you never know how many people you will reach indirectly through helping just one person.

Thanks to my speaking engagements, I've inspired many people to start speaking themselves and create more impact through live events. Thanks to sharing my story, I have inspired people, helped them get through their depression and anxiety, and even saved some lives from suicide, and I want to save a whole lot more.

Combining my story with my charity and online education programs, I aim to save many millions more.

On average, someone takes their own life every forty seconds. Over 700,000 people each year reach such a dark place that they don't make it out. And that number doesn't even take into account the people who survive, like me. Sadly, that means by the time you have finished this book, more than 225 lives will have been lost to this plague.

There is a pandemic that has been growing exponentially around the world for years that is much bigger than COVID-19. And that is the mental health pandemic. The more I share my story with people around the world, the more I realize how many people suffer with anxiety, depression, social phobia, and other debilitating mental health disorders.

The amount of people will shock you. Over 70 percent of the thousands of people I speak to about mental health have suffered in some way, shape, or form.

There are more and more people suffering in silence because of how *taboo* it is to talk about it.

The thing is, we are not alone at all. In fact, the people who *don't* suffer some form of mental health issues are in the minority! In 2019, suicide was the fourth leading cause of death among fifteen-to-twenty-nine-year-olds *globally*, and I am guessing that number has risen substantially since then, considering the stresses of 2020 and beyond.

One of the leading risk factors for suicide is feeling alone and like there's no one to talk to.

This is especially true for men.

We are supposed to hide our feelings and suck it up, because according to society, men aren't men if they have these feelings.

Bullshit.

It is perfectly natural to have and talk about these feelings. It doesn't mean there is anything wrong with you or that you have weird wiring. It means you're human—and a decent one at that, because you actually give a damn!

Our society still stigmatizes these feelings and thoughts, but until that taboo is lifted and we all feel safe to talk about it, I don't believe things will improve.

My mission is to break the silence and the taboo around mental health struggles and let people know they are not alone. They have someone to talk to without fear of being judged.

We can debate about and try and fight the root causes as much as you wish, but people are still going to post the best bits of their life on social media and hide the ugly, making viewers feel inadequate. People are still going to have different upbringings and feel inferior to people with more than them. Some people are still going to get abused, and some people are going to feel some kind of way sometimes.

The most important thing around mental health is not prevention.

Yes, we should try to prevent hurt and abuse as much as we can, but not to the point of coddling and raising a society so weak, its people crumble at the first sign of hardship. If you try too hard to prevent mental health issues, you end up causing more. If you constantly protect people, they grow up weak and soft, deriving meaning from comfort, and when the crap does eventually hit the fan, they all want to kill themselves because they're so ill-equipped for it.

It's not about making sure bad things don't happen. It's about opening up and letting people know it is okay and safe to talk about their struggles without fear.

Sharing my story is my first step toward that, and my hope is that it inspires many more to do the same.

I plan to open my own charity that will help break the silence around mental health, make it a less taboo subject, help people find a safe space to open up, and then sponsor people who are ready to learn about entrepreneurship and working from home.

If you or someone else is suffering in silence, I beg you to talk to someone about it and be brutally honest about how you feel. Carrying it around without anyone to talk to is the most destructive thing you can do.

I know this firsthand because it is what I did for a long time. I was bitter, angry, resentful, and constantly full of anguish. It was only when I started to talk about it that the pain started to subside.

As you know, I have a lot of regrets in my life. I'm sure you do too. The feeling of regret is the biggest pain I have ever felt. One of the biggest things that keeps me pushing forward and becoming better is the drive to avoid that pain as much as possible.

Things aren't perfect; they never will be. I still struggle like crazy in social situations, and I am still terrified of being around new people, especially women. I still get that sinking feeling in my chest and PTSD reactions when I hear loud noises at night, because it reminds me of people breaking into my home. I still have tons of repressed memories from my childhood not mentioned in this book that subconsciously drive my actions.

Yet as dysfunctional as I am, I have still, by anyone's metrics, done pretty darn well for myself over the last few years and continue to be the best I can every single day, despite my setbacks.

Too many people become victims of their circumstances and use that victim mentality as an excuse for settling for less than what they are capable of.

They wait for things to be perfect before taking action, or they avoid change altogether. I know this because I did the exact same thing for years.

If you live your life waiting for things to be perfect, then you will be waiting until the day you die.

I wish I had documented my thought process since I survived the overdose, but I do know this: there's only one step to success.

Desire.

A burning desire to make a change.

The desire to make a change more than anything else.

The desire to make something of yourself.

The desire to overcome the mental laziness that is instilled in most people's minds.

When you really desire to make a change, when you are sick of things staying the same, when you have the desire to continue even after you hit a brick wall...

You will succeed.

The *only* thing that separates the successful from the unsuccessful is their desire to make a change and to keep attacking it, no matter how many times they fail.

As you grow and start to see results, there will be people who want to see you fail. Some people may troll you, discredit you, put you down, and even downright lie to try and damage your reputation. It's tempting to put them in their place and expose them, but it doesn't feel good to do.

Sadly, the more success you create, the more jealousy and animosity you will create, too. Apart from it being ethical, this is the main reason you need to be honest and true to everything you say. The bigger you get, the more people will try and hurt you. Don't give them any ammunition!

Some people may not like something you say. Some people may want to compete with you and bring you down. Some people will be jealous. And others may just be colossal douche monkeys.

Whatever the reason, don't let them bring you down and stop you pushing forward. Because it's when we encounter the most resistance that we can know we are about to reach the next level. Keep pushing forward, and never give up.

For me, starting my own business—first to prove to myself that I could and wasn't a loser, and then to make an impact in the world—is what helped me climb out of the mental health hole I was living in. That business has changed my life.

Maybe you have no desire to build your own business and are quite happy working for someone else. If that's you, kudos! For me, there's no feeling more rewarding than building my own dream instead of someone else's. If you are the same—if you have a vision, a dream, and a craving for true freedom—then there is nothing that should stop you from pursuing that.

You don't need to all-out attack it every waking moment like I did, although you will succeed much faster if you do. If your circumstances and commitments prevent you from going all in right now, then start part-time until you are able to free up more time.

If you feel like you have no time, then search your life for something you can cut out. It could be TV, video games, an unhealthy relationship, or even an hour of sleep every night. Just remember it is temporary, and when you succeed, you will have way more time to yourself.

I sacrificed all my time for a few years to now have a freedom most can only dream of. I now have way more free time and resources, and if you ask me if it was worth it, I would tell you, "Heck yes!"

Only you can decide what is worth sacrificing to achieve ultimate freedom.

As of 2022, it has never been easier to build a business online. Since the COVID-19 pandemic, we have realized we don't have to stay where we are, and there are more avenues open to us to work online. Of course, this also means there has never been so much noise and competition in the marketplace as there is right now.

But there are some paths that are easier for beginners than others. One of these is affiliate marketing, which helped me build my seven-figure business. I've said this already, but it's worth repeating: I believe affiliate marketing is the best and easiest business model for anyone. I believe it is especially useful for someone who may not yet be equipped to deal with the higher-stress business models out there. It's also a perfect stepping stone to greater things later should you choose to progress.

You must remember, though, this is not a get-rich-quick, push-button business model. They don't exist—trust me, I've looked very hard!

The strategies I teach have the ability to earn you hundreds of thousands and even millions of dollars, but it is not going to happen overnight. There are so many schemes and false promises out there that are just that—false. I've been around the block a few times in the online world and am disgusted at the number of false promises, scams, and rip-off merchants sullying the space today by promising quick riches. Getting rich quickly only happens at someone else's expense or in extraordinary circumstances and requires an inordinate amount of luck, just like the lottery.

Unfortunately, as I was writing this book, one of the biggest crypto projects collapsed, and many people lost their life savings to what they had thought was going to be a get-rich-quick plan. The only get-rich-quick plan I know of that is legitimate is a form of gambling, through and through.

Affiliate marketing, however, is not a gamble. It is a way to build high-paying skills and income streams that pay us long after we have done the work. It is very possible to replace your job, benefits, and any other income you have relatively quickly with persistence and dedication, but if you treat it like a hobby, it is going to pay like a hobby.

When I decided I wasn't going to allow myself to gain any more weight, I ultimately lost over fifty pounds. It's taken a lot of discipline and energy to get there.

Business is exactly the same.

When I first started, I plugged away for six months with zero payoff. There was no sign of any progress at all. Yet in that sixth month, the money started to come in. When you first start, you're not likely to see results in a day, a week, or a month. It's a gradual progression, but if you stick with it, you're going to see everything start to crystallize.

Sadly, many people reading this message will quit on day five, week five, or month five, just before they're about to see results...and the effort they put in will be for nothing. If someone sticks with affiliate marketing, it is literally impossible to fail.

I don't know many other business models where you can make as much money so fast. I started from absolutely nothing in 2017. I had never done any marketing in my entire life, and within the first three years, I built a six-figure income that puts me in the top 10 percent of earners worldwide and close to the top 5 percent of earners in the US.

Think about how long it takes to get a six-figure income through traditional education and employment. Some people spend five or even ten years training for a traditional high-paying job. What I have done over the past few years and what I can teach you to do is build an online business in an area where people consistently become six- and seven-figure earners.

Now, what's even more amazing and why I truly think affiliate marketing is the best business model in the world is that the income I have built up is now recurring. I promote mainly membership-based products, so the money I have coming in right now is automatic. I did the work once, I connected the person who needed the service to the person who could provide the service, and now I get paid for the lifetime of the customer.

I can literally close my laptop and stop right now, and the money would keep rolling in. Yes I had to put in a lot of up-front work, but I do not anymore.

Are you starting to see how powerful this is and why I think it is the best business model in the world? It's truly a freeing, amazing feeling to know that at any moment, I can just take a month off to do nothing and keep getting paid. Heck, I wouldn't have been able to handle product creation, fulfillment, support, and all of that other icky stuff when I first began. Affiliate marketing was a perfect stepping stone for me to get started when my skills and social abilities were at an all-time low, which is why I recommend it to beginners.

It also gave me a chance to get great at selling products online without having to worry about anything else. When the time came to create my own products, I was far more comfortable selling and marketing.

You just heard my story. I am nothing special. After years of locking myself away playing video games, my confidence and social skills were terrible. I could barely look anyone in the eye, let alone hold a conversation. I could tell you the entire five-thousand-year fictional history of the Elder Scrolls (a popular role-playing game), but I couldn't name one of the last five presidents or prime ministers.

I had nothing to talk about and no value to give.

So before you tell yourself you can't do what I've done, think back on my story. I was staring down at the bottom of a pill bottle in 2017. Are you in a worse position today?

If you would like to learn more about affiliate marketing and perhaps pursue it yourself, scan the following QR code, and I will send you a premium training on the basics of affiliate marketing for free.

Consider it my gift to you for sticking with me and hearing my story.

I really hope this book has opened your eyes to what is possible with persistence, faith, and a desire to make a change. I appreciate you, and I hope my story has affected you in at least some small way.

I'd love to hear your story, especially if you have not shared it with anyone else before. Like I said, opening up and talking about our struggles is an important first step—even writing it out can have a profound effect on the healing process.

I would love to hear your feedback and takeaways. I would love to hear how my story has impacted you and the people around you. I would love to hear your questions.

As a valued reader who now knows me better than most, I would love to hear from you in any way, shape, or form.

Please send an email to book@tayloryourbestlife.com to get in touch.

Acknowledgments

Mum, we've had our ups and downs and come out the other side. Despite our challenges, you always knew I was capable of greatness, even when I didn't see it in myself. Thanks for doing the best you could with the hand you were dealt.

Erick Salgado, your advice and friendship have helped me get to where I am today. I consider you not only a very close friend, but also part of my family. You are one of the best male role models I've ever had. You always do the right thing, even when nobody's looking, and you are an example of what every great leader should be.

Shelly Turner, since we met in 2017, you have been a great friend. Your giving of your time and your willingness to help everyone is admirable. Whenever I needed advice or just someone to talk to, you were there. Thank you for being a true friend.

Dan Meredith, you are an awesome mate and amazing mentor. Thanks so much for being an ear when I needed it and helping bring this book to life. Your recommended therapeutics have helped restore my health and enjoyment in life.

Angus Buckle, you are an amazing performance coach and health mentor. Thanks for your support in building my health and fitness levels to my best ever. Your sleep coaching has helped me gain many more hours every week.

Omar and Melinda Martin, without your presence in my life in 2022, I don't know where I would be. I truly believe divine intervention brought us together just in time to see me through a very turbulent time. Thank you.

Tom Beal, thank you for being a true friend and great mentor. I have learned so much from you, and you have always been there with great insights when I needed advice.

Henry Gold, thank you for teaching me the importance of the power of one. Without you, I would never have launched my own programs or helped thousands of people break free from the shackles of mediocrity and earn a living online. My experience with you encapsulates the power of one.

To everyone who has been a part of my journey, small or large, thank you! There are too many to list here, and I thank you all from the bottom of my heart for being who you are.

About the Author

James Neville-Taylor is a self-made millionaire who clawed his way up from the depths of despair.

After surviving childhood emotional, physical, and sexual abuse and numerous suicide attempts, he found a light in the darkness that gave him a new lease on life.

Within just one year of his final suicide attempt, he built a successful business and quickly became an international speaker and mental health advocate, speaking on stages across North America, South America, and Europe.

He is an award-winning product creator and affiliate marketer, having claimed multiple awards, including a brand-new car in a 2019 competition.

Today, James travels the world as an advocate for mental health, completely supported by his online income. He shares his story to inspire, motivate, and teach people to "Taylor Their Best Life."

To learn more about James and his journey, visit:
https://tayloryourbestlife.com.

Printed in Great Britain
by Amazon